# Cooking with a Plan®
## Volume I
## Back to the Kitchen
### Andy Anderson

*Burnt Toast Publications*
*Wichita, Kansas*
*www.realandy.com*

Burnt Toast Publications®
Subsidiary of One-of-a-Kind Productions, Inc®
534 Brookfield, Wichita, Kansas 67206-1518
1.316.684.3456 - http://www.realandy.com

Text and photography © 2008. Food styling by Andy Anderson/Bonnie Loyd.

All rights reserved. No part of this book may be reproduced, stored, introduced into a retrieval system, or otherwise copied in any form without the prior written permission of the publisher, except for brief quotations in reviews or citations.

Library of Congress Cataloging-in-Publication Data
Anderson, Andy
Cooking with a Plan Vol I: Back to the Kitchen / Andy Anderson
p. cm. Cooking with a Plan Series
ISBN-13: 978-0-6152-0227-3 (pbk.)

Photography created using a Nikon D2Xs, processed using Adobe Photoshop CS3.
Illustrations created using Adobe Illustrator CS3.
Additional images and clipart: www.clipart.com, www.iStock.com, www.digitaljuice.com.
Document layout created in Adobe InDesign CS3, and then distilled to PDF using Adobe Acrobat 8.
Major font: ITC Benguiat BT.

# Does the World Really need another Cookbook...

Actually, that's a pretty fair question... Does the world really need another cookbook?

There are probably more cookbooks in bookstores than any other genre (I just made that up, but it does sound plausible). Just go to the bookstore and check it out for yourself... rows upon rows of cookbooks on every conceivable topic. Cookbooks to lose weight, cookbooks to gain weight, cookbooks for healthy eating, and cookbooks on unhealthy eating; even cookbooks with recipes for your pets. As a matter of fact, if you ever find your way to Roswell, New Mexico, they even have cookbooks with recipes from extraterrestrial cultures (Martian stew was my personal favorite).

So that leads us back to the main question: Does the world really need another cookbook? If you're asking me, then the answer is, yes (you didn't really expect me to say no, did you), and here's my reasoning.

I'm a graphic's designer and animator with a passion for cooking. You might even say I was born to it. I studied in Europe, and in the United States, and worked at several restaurants here and abroad. However, I found out that working 8 to 10 hours a day in a hot kitchen was not my idea of cooking. Restaurant cooking is a bit mechanical. Sure you're preparing great meals; however, you wind up being isolated all day in the kitchen. To me, cooking is about preparing great meals for my family and friends... in other words: Entertaining. Fortunately, all that studying in culinary schools was not wasted, because it taught me the foundations of great cooking.

This book is not simply a book of recipes; it's a book of how you organize yourself. I want to teach you how to master the kitchen. And if you master the kitchen, you will master the recipes.

Now, at this point you're probably saying something like: "Oh no, not an organizational book with flowcharts, and graphs.".

Let me ask you a question: Have you ever been halfway through a recipe, only to find out that you're missing a key ingredient? Or, you're hosting an outdoor BBQ, and you discover (as you begin cooking) that you're out of charcoal, or propane? Do you constantly have your guests running to the store to pick up that essential item?

Think of how that all changes when you know you've got what you need to get the job done; you've planned it out, and you're ready to rock. Most people think that culinary schools are just about cooking; however, they are much more than that... they are about planning, and knowing how.

This book is intended to help you with your kitchen skills by employing, what I call the six steps to culinary success: Plan, Purchase, Prep, Prepare, Plate, & Present. And after that, some really great recipes to get you started.

So, does the world really need another cookbook... I suspect that in the end that question must ultimately be answered by you.

But I hope your answer is, yes.

# Why I Cook

Why does anyone do what they do?
To me cooking isn't a chore, it's a grand opportunity to share my talents as a chef with my friends and family. My philosophy is simple: since we have to eat every day, it might as well be a fun thing to do.
I cook not because I have to, but because I choose to, and that's a big difference.
Cooking is fun, and it's an excellent way to unite people together.
Enjoy this book, and may it help to remind you of the importance of family, and how much fun it is to break bread together.

Remember… Friends don't let friends eat alone.

Share the Joy, & Enjoy the Journey

Andy Anderson

# Dedication

Dedications are always a bit dicey, simply because they only mean something to the person or persons receiving the honor of the dedication. With that said, I've written 18 books to date, and they always begin with the person that I share my life with… Bonnie, you helped me become the person I am with your love and support. I can't image a world without you and your loving smile in it. Thank you for being a significant part of my life. You are my wife, my partner, my lover, and my friend. As to others… there are always others, I want to thank my Aunt Josephine for encouraging my love of cooking when I was just a lad of nine, and guiding my feet on the culinary path.

And as always, I want to thank Herb Tarlic Jr., and Lovejoy, our two Jack Russell terriers. For being there with their unconditional love, and for their willingness to taste test some of these recipes.

# A Personal Philosophy of Cooking

Allow me to share with you my philosophy of what great cooking is all about...

I am not attempting to create what is known as "fast" food. The philosophy of quick cooking I will leave for other writers and television shows.

When it come to cooking, we've lost something in our fast-paced society. We have lost the love and pure joy of cooking. In years past, cooking meant something quite different than what it means today. Cooking was not just sitting down at the table, it was so much more than that. Cooking involves food, and food is life... and life is something to be enjoyed.

I was blessed with a father that loved to cook, and an Italian aunt who, also, loved to cook. When I was growing up in Chicago (as a lad) I watched my dad and aunt cook and, when I spent weekends with my aunt, not only would I watch her cook, she would let me help her. Early on in life, I learned the joys that are a part of cooking.

When my Aunt Josephine worked in the kitchen, she wasn't alone... Over the course of the day, family and friends would come in and out of the kitchen, talk , and would even help in the preparation of the meal. The cooking of the meal was just as important as the eating of the meal. That's not to say, that my aunt spent the entire day cooking, but when she was in the kitchen, it wasn't a taboo place for others to congregate. It was as much the "living room" as any other room in the house.

When the meal was ready, everyone sat around the table, talked, laughed, and enjoyed each other's company. The meal was only a part of the process. I don't want to make meals in the shortest time possible, I don't want to hasten the process. I enjoy cooking, and my friends and relatives enjoy being a part of the process (well, most of relatives enjoy the process). As someone once said, it's not the destination; it's the journey... Now that was a wise dude.

Today, we fast-process, microwave, and TV dinner our meals. Then we sit down, eat without conversation, and move on to other (more important) things. It shouldn't be that way... it wasn't intended to be that way.

Try something like this... once a week, or once a month, spend a portion of the day working on the creation of a meal. Invite friends and family over... talk, have fun, and then enjoy life. I guarantee you'll have a great time.

Remember, it's not about the meal, it's about the one's you share it with... enjoy.

# The Plan

| | |
|---|---:|
| Control | 26 |
| Plan | 34 |
| Purchase | 36 |
| Prep | 38 |
| Prepare | 40 |
| Plate | 42 |
| Present | 44 |
| Summary | 44 |

# Eggs & Such

Fantastic French Toast . . . . . . . . . . . 48
Sausage/Egg Casserole Surprise . . . . . . 49
Southwest Eggs & Chili . . . . . . . . . . 50
Awesome Breakfast Burritos . . . . . . . . 51
Awesome Buttermilk Biscuits . . . . . . . 52
Homemade Breakfast Sausage . . . . . . . 53
Made From Scratch Granola . . . . . . . . 54
A Proper British Breakfast . . . . . . . . 55
To Die For Waffles . . . . . . . . . . . . 56
Unique Baked Omelet . . . . . . . . . . . 57
Creamy Scrambled Eggs . . . . . . . . . . 58

# Appetizers

Crusted Goat Cheese Medallions . . . . . . . . . . 62
Baked Green Olives & Cheese . . . . . . . . . . . 63
Cheese & Apples . . . . . . . . . . . . . . . . . 64
Crab Rangoon . . . . . . . . . . . . . . . . . . 65
Stuffed Mushrooms . . . . . . . . . . . . . . . . 66
Cucumber Sandwiches . . . . . . . . . . . . . . . 67
Cocktail Meatballs . . . . . . . . . . . . . . . 68
Baked Potato Skins . . . . . . . . . . . . . . . 69
Awesome Guacamole . . . . . . . . . . . . . . . . 70
Not So Classic Spinach Dip . . . . . . . . . . . 71

# Beef & Pork

Tasty Corned Beef . . . . . . . . . . . . . . . 74
Ultimate Stuffed Pork Chops. . . . . . . . . . . 75
Korean Barbecued Beef . . . . . . . . . . . . . 76
Melt-in-Your-Mouth Pork Roast. . . . . . . . . . 77
Stick-to-your-ribs Irish Stew . . . . . . . . . 78
Tender Beef Tips. . . . . . . . . . . . . . . . 79
Beef and Pepper Saute . . . . . . . . . . . . . 80
Shepherd's Pie. . . . . . . . . . . . . . . . . 81
Pork Ribs Texas Style . . . . . . . . . . . . . 82
Slow Cooked Beef Stew . . . . . . . . . . . . . 83

# Poultry

French Style Chicken in a Pot . . . . . . . . . . . 86
Chicken Papadoris . . . . . . . . . . . . . . . . . . 87
Saltimbocca . . . . . . . . . . . . . . . . . . . . . . 88
Rotisserie Style Chicken . . . . . . . . . . . . . . 89
Mouth Watering Cilantro Chicken . . . . . . . . 90
Chicken Cordon Bleu . . . . . . . . . . . . . . . . 91
Pasta & Chicken . . . . . . . . . . . . . . . . . . . 92
Chicken Piccata . . . . . . . . . . . . . . . . . . . 93
Garlic Chicken . . . . . . . . . . . . . . . . . . . . 94
Sesame & Teriyaki Chicken Wings . . . . . . . . 95

# Fish

Drunken Salmon . . . . . . . . . . . . . . . . . . . . . . 98
East Coast Crab Cakes . . . . . . . . . . . . . . . . . . 99
Baked Fish . . . . . . . . . . . . . . . . . . . . . . . . . 100
Fish Tacos . . . . . . . . . . . . . . . . . . . . . . . . . 101
Fish Meuniere . . . . . . . . . . . . . . . . . . . . . . 102
Grilled Tilapia . . . . . . . . . . . . . . . . . . . . . . 103
Cilantro and Tomato Seafood Bake . . . . . . . . 104
Spicy Fish Cakes . . . . . . . . . . . . . . . . . . . . 105
Pan Roasted Halibut . . . . . . . . . . . . . . . . . 106
Baked Salmon . . . . . . . . . . . . . . . . . . . . . 107

# Side Dishes

Awesome Garlic Mash Potatoes . . . . . . . . . . . . . . . . . . . 110
Pommes Anna . . . . . . . . . . . . . . . . . . . . . . . . . . . . 111
Broccoli Casserole . . . . . . . . . . . . . . . . . . . . . . . . 112
Fried Rice . . . . . . . . . . . . . . . . . . . . . . . . . . . . 113
Candied Sweet Potatoes . . . . . . . . . . . . . . . . . . . . . . 114
Fantasic Green Beans . . . . . . . . . . . . . . . . . . . . . . . 115
Baked Beans . . . . . . . . . . . . . . . . . . . . . . . . . . . . 116
Spanish Rice . . . . . . . . . . . . . . . . . . . . . . . . . . . 117
Mushroom Risotto . . . . . . . . . . . . . . . . . . . . . . . . . 118
Roasted Vegetables . . . . . . . . . . . . . . . . . . . . . . . . 119

# Sweets

Scottish Shortbread . . . . . . . . . . . . . . . . . . . . . . . . 122
Coconut Macaroons . . . . . . . . . . . . . . . . . . . . . . . 123
Classic Apple Pie . . . . . . . . . . . . . . . . . . . . . . . . . 124
Deep Dish Brownies . . . . . . . . . . . . . . . . . . . . . . 125
Carrot Cake . . . . . . . . . . . . . . . . . . . . . . . . . . . . . 126
Mango Coconut Parfait . . . . . . . . . . . . . . . . . . . 127
Pecan Coffee Cake . . . . . . . . . . . . . . . . . . . . . . . 128
Pecan Lace Cookies . . . . . . . . . . . . . . . . . . . . . . 129
Pecan Pralines . . . . . . . . . . . . . . . . . . . . . . . . . . 130
Apple Crisp . . . . . . . . . . . . . . . . . . . . . . . . . . . . 131

# Soups

Hearty Beef Chili . . . . . . . . . . . . . . . . . . . . . 134
Hamburger Vegetable Soup . . . . . . . . . . . . . 135
Poached Garlic Soup . . . . . . . . . . . . . . . . . . 136
Clam Chowder . . . . . . . . . . . . . . . . . . . . . . 137
Potato Soup Supreme . . . . . . . . . . . . . . . . . 138
Butternut Squash Soup . . . . . . . . . . . . . . . . 139
Chicken Noodle Soup . . . . . . . . . . . . . . . . . 140
Tomato Bisque . . . . . . . . . . . . . . . . . . . . . . 141
French Onion Soup . . . . . . . . . . . . . . . . . . 142
Broccoli Soup . . . . . . . . . . . . . . . . . . . . . . 143

# Sandwiches & Salads

Midnight Sandwiches . . . . . . . . . . . . . . . .146
Tempting Tuna Salad . . . . . . . . . . . . . . . .147
Roast Turkey Panini . . . . . . . . . . . . . . . .148
Ham & Cheese Baguettes . . . . . . . . . . . . . .149
Super Burgers . . . . . . . . . . . . . . . . . . .150
Not So Boring Potato Salad . . . . . . . . . . . .151
Grilled Veggie Sandwich . . . . . . . . . . . . . .152
Pulled Beef Sandwiches . . . . . . . . . . . . . .153
Classic Caesar Salad . . . . . . . . . . . . . . .154
Mandarin Orange Spring Salad . . . . . . . . . . .155

# Stocks, Broths & Sauces

Chunky Cherry Tomato Sauce . . . . . . . . . . . .158
Homemade Chicken Stock . . . . . . . . . . . . .159
Building a Raft . . . . . . . . . . . . . . . . . . .160
Pineapple Reduction . . . . . . . . . . . . . . . .161
Butter-Sage Sauce . . . . . . . . . . . . . . . . .162
Thyme and Red Pepper Cream . . . . . . . . . . .163
Classic Marinara . . . . . . . . . . . . . . . . . .164
Flavorful Beef Stock . . . . . . . . . . . . . . . .165
Down Home BBQ Sauce . . . . . . . . . . . . . .166
Awesome Alfredo Sauce . . . . . . . . . . . . . .167

# About this Book
## Definitions & Such

There are several things to remember when working with the recipes in this book... for that matter, the recipes in any cookbook.

First of all, you should always read a recipe completely through before starting. While that may seem like a simple matter, many budding chefs simply grab the recipe, and begin working from the first step... only to find out that in step 4 they're missing an essential ingredient (I hate it when that happens).

Of course, if you're following the Plan, you won't have that problem... now will you.

## Abbreviations

| | | |
|---|---|---|
| T. | = | tablespoon(s) |
| t. | = | teaspoon(s) |
| c. | = | cup(s) |
| oz. | = | ounce(s) |
| lb. | = | pound(s) |
| pt. | = | pint(s) |
| qt. | = | quart(s) |
| gal. | = | gallon(s) |

When the term salt is used by itself, it refers to ordinary table salt (*like Morton's, When It Rains, It Pours, salt*).

## Recipes

All of the recipes in this book have been tried and tested by myself, and others. They're an eclectic mix of good recipes with lots of punch and flavor. Although many of the recipes are fairly easy to make, most take a bit of time to prepare.

As stated earlier, the purpose of the book is not to give you meals-in-a-minute; it's geared to cooks and chefs who, like myself, enjoy creating great meals, entertaining with friends and family, and just plain having fun in the kitchen. Golfers enjoy a good game of golf with their friends. There's a challenge to the game, and there's a creative way it's played that can only be understood by someone who loves the game of golf... That's who this book and these recipes are geared toward... the lover of the game.

My personal motto: **Anything Worth Doing, Is Worth Overdoing...**

# All Journeys begin with the first step...

In the case of cooking great meals that will wow your guests, the first step is planning. Some people are born to plan, and some people have planning thrust upon them (OUCH).

If I were to be honest, I would probably have to say that the idea of planning grew on me. I discovered that planning helps to alleviate the strain and frustration that sometimes goes hand-in-hand with going into the kitchen; especially if you don't have any clear idea of what you want to accomplish. It's like taking a vacation without any clear idea as to how you're going to get to your destination. If you don't know your destination, how are you ever going to know when you arrive?

When I attended cooking classes, I was amazed to discover that we didn't just jump in and start cooking. Our instructor/chefs had us go over the kitchen, understand where everything was, or as the French say: Mise en place (mi z ˈplas]), literally translated from French, means "setting in place." The chefs at the Culinary Institute of America (CIA) describe the term as "Everything in place". When you're preparing a meal, it's used to describe the preparation done before starting the actual cooking process, or what I call, The Plan.

Talking with a heavy German accent, our instructor would say, you can't be a good chef without knowing the layout of your kitchen. Occasionally, he would stop and ask one of us where a certain piece of equipment was located. He might shout out: Where's my zester? And woe to the student that hesitated with his or her response.

Over the years I came up with an organizational scheme that helps to plan out anything from a lunch for two (or one), to a massive dinner party. The following chart gives you a general idea of how the plan goes:

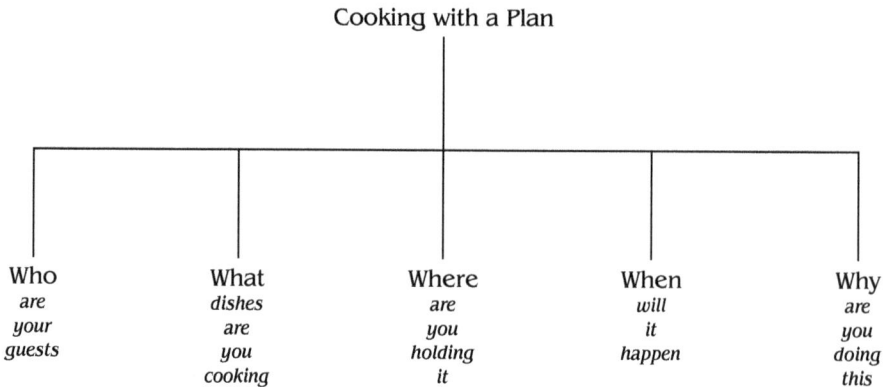

All great culinary experiences begin with a solid plan

# The Power of the Process...

Okay, let's get up front and honest about this whole thing. If you're a professional chef, you already understand the necessity of planning through a meal; however, if you haven't spent your entire life cranking out meal after meal with some nasty face sous chef breathing down your neck (sorry, just had a flash back), you might feel like the planning of a meal is a bit of overkill for your particular situation. If that's how you feel, then you might want to rethink that position.

A good plan gives you a feeling of control, and in any situation control is a good thing. That sense of control gives you more confidence; possibly to go where you've never gone before. Finally, that confidence leads to you being more creative.

The more you practice the Plan, the easier it becomes, the more fun you're going to have in the kitchen, the more meals you're going to want to cook, and the more entertaining you're going to want to do.

So buckle up, put your tray tables and seat backs into their upright and locked position. Get ready to take off on the adventure of a lifetime... it's the power of The Plan (I was going to call it The Secret, but I heard that name was already taken).

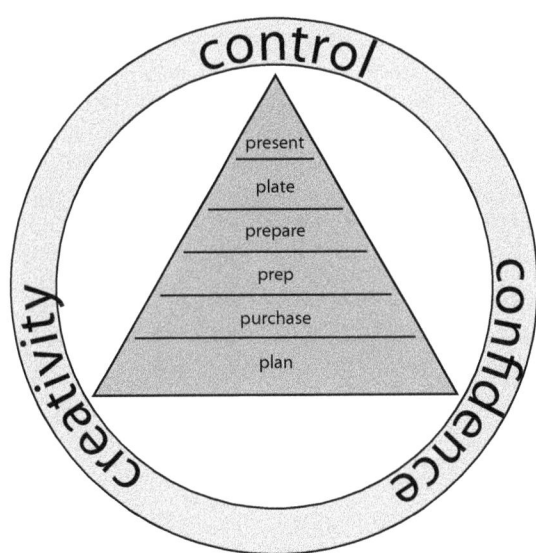

# Six Essential Steps to Culinary Success

Control of your kitchen can be broken down into six simple steps: Plan, Purchase, Prep, Prepare, Plate, and Present. You can further group the steps into a logical process; therefore Planning and Purchasing go together, as do Prepping and Preparing, the final two steps Plating and Presenting complete the process. So, if six steps are a bit much, you can look at it as three steps with two divisions per step (I sincerely hope that makes you feel better).

The first part of this book will deal with the process of controlling your kitchen by the use of The Plan, and the rest of the book contains over 100 mouth-watering recipes that you can use to practice The Plan.

The appendixes of this book contain culinary definitions, as well as some sample recipe cards and charts that you can use. Feel free to make copies, or possibly come up with your own working system. Ultimately, the system that works the best for you, is the one that you're most comfortable using.

### A word of advice:

As you begin cooking and creating your own recipes, you will find that having a good organizational system is a tremendous help. For example, I have thousands of recipes that I used to have on index cards; faithfully cataloged in little tin boxes (raise your hand, if you use the same system). Over the last few years, I've transferred those recipes to a cooking database that I created. Each recipe has a specific number. Now, when I'm planning a party, I select the recipes needed by number, and then print them out. In addition, the program also prints out a shopping list of related items. I will admit that being a geek, did help in the creation of the application; however, that aside, it makes my life of finding the recipes I need, and creating a shopping list (the first stage of planning) a whole lot easier.

So, if you'll turn the page, we'll begin the process by describing some essential kitchen skills, and then it's on to the Plan.

After that there are over 100 mouth-watering recipes just waiting for you to practice on…

Just remember to have fun.

PLAN

PURCHASE

PREP

Prepare

Plate

Present

# Control

## Knowledge is Power

Before we get started on the six steps of creating a meal, there is something you need to do before anything else... **Control your kitchen**. I'm not talking about the cooking process (that comes later), I'm talking about knowing where things are when you need them.

If you're lucky enough to have a big kitchen, then you have plenty of drawer and cabinet space to put all your stuff (I have a lot of stuff). Unfortunately, that also means you have a lot of space to lose stuff, or better yet, forget you ever had it.

Once upon a time, when I was doing a lot of carving for a catering job, I decided that I needed a bird's beak knife. I was about to go to the local Williams-Sonoma (great place to shop), when, I opened my knife drawer for a quick peek. Hidden in the corner was a brand spanking new Henckels bird's beak (Henckels is my knife of choice). At the time, I didn't need it, so it went into the drawer... out of sight, out of mind. I was about to drop a hundred bucks on a knife I already owned. That also means that all the peeling and carving I had been doing for a catering project, would have gone much faster, if I only knew about that knife.

Organize your workspace the way a professional chef organizes his or her workspace. As mentioned earlier, the French say: Mise en place (mi z ˈplas]), "setting in place." Or, a place for everything, and everything in its place.

Here's a thought: Kitchen drawers are not just for throwing things into, they should have some semblance of organization. For example, never just toss your precious knifes into a drawer; they should be kept in a counter-top butcher block holder, or drawer organizer. I use a drawer organizer, for my knifes, and the other area of the drawer is occupied with the tools I use most often. I have a second drawer that contains tools I use, but not as often. And I have a third drawer that contains tools I want handy, but I only use once in a blue moon (I've never seen a blue moon, so they must be really rare).

To further organize the drawers, I went to Bed, Bath, & Beyond and picked up some drawer organizers. Hey, why not, they're always sending me these 20-percent off coupons in the mail, so I figured it was time to go shopping.

# Just a Wee Bit of Pre Planning

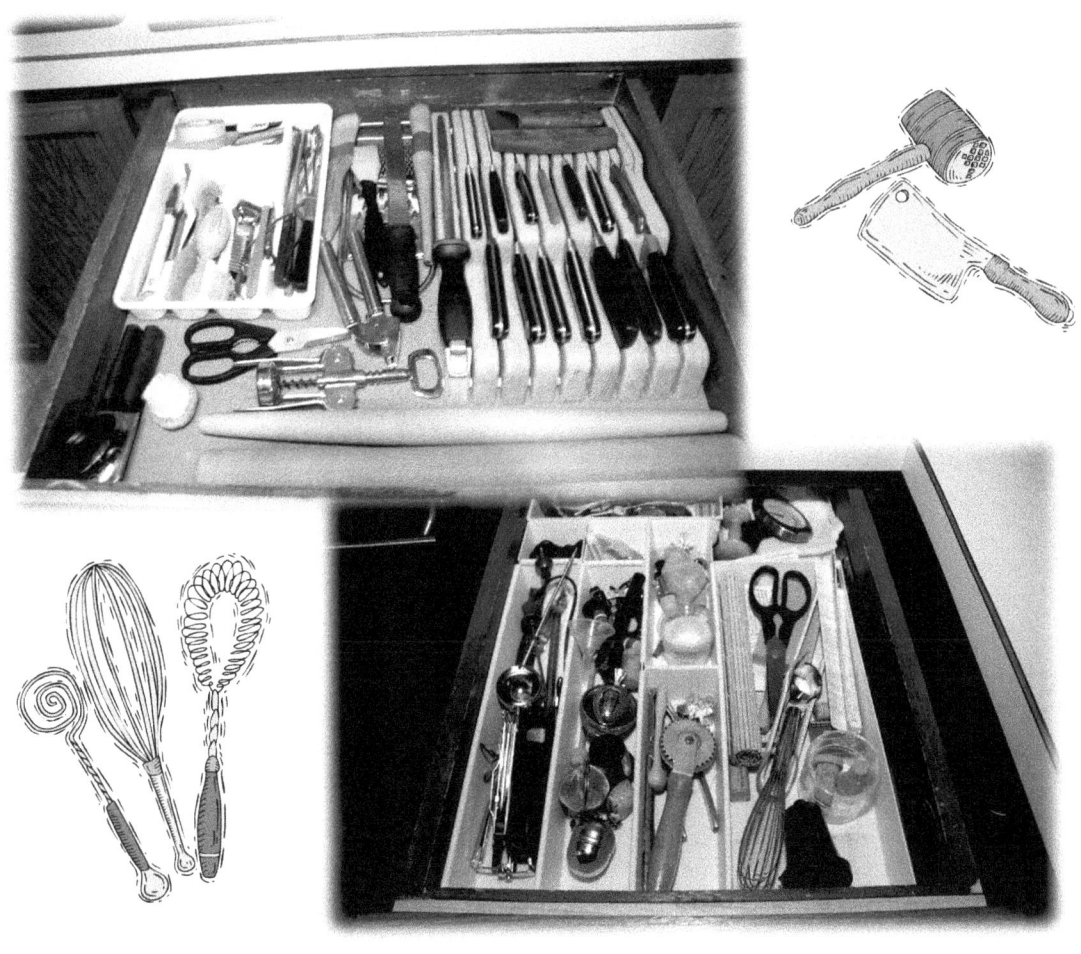

Mise en place

# Control

## Control

### *Knowledge is Power*

I've been asked this question more than once: Do you have to get this organized to have fun in the kitchen? Not really, actually it depends on exactly what level of retentive you are. On a scale of 1 to 10 (10 being the most retentive), I put myself conservatively at a 12. To me, walking into my kitchen and knowing that everything is where it's supposed to be is part of the fun. However, everybody has a level where the idea of organization is taken to an extreme; where it's no longer about being creative and having fun... it's all about the organization. If organization is not your thing, take heart and listen to the words of one of my former instructors, as he spoke to his fledgling chefs:

> *"It's not necessary to be so organized that you squeeze all the fun out of cooking. Simply choose an organizational scheme that works best for you. So wherever you choose to put your tools... you will know where they are, and be able to access them quickly."*

Those are words of wisdom...

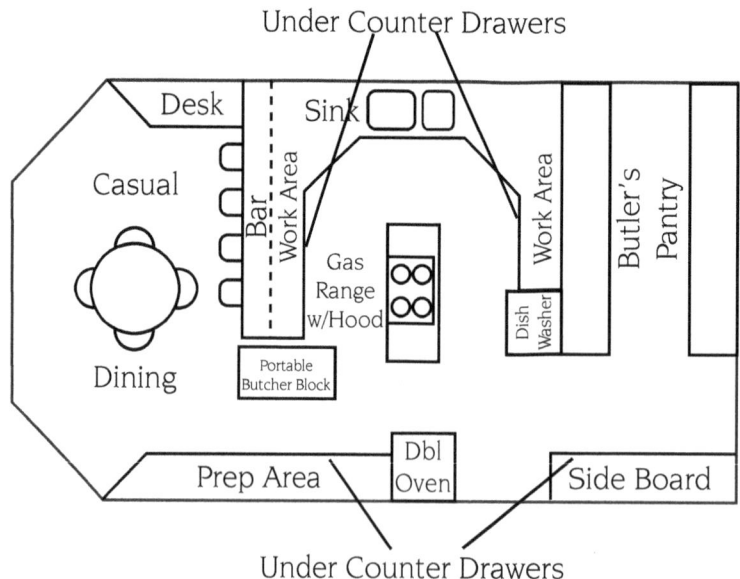

# The Story Before the Plan

Prep & Measure

Sugar & Spice

Pots & Pans

# Step 1: Planning

## *Every journey begins with the first step*

Planning typically involves forethought. For example, if I'm planning a large dinner party on the weekend, I might begin planning the meal a week or more before the event. As a matter of fact, since we do big holiday dinners, I begin planning Thanksgiving and Christmas two or more months ahead of the events. With that said, I have been known to enter the kitchen an hour before dinner, stick my head in the refrigerator, and begin hunting around for something to fix. Such is the way of life.

Typically, I plan family dinners a week at a time (on Sunday evening), and consult with my wife on the nightly selections. Once the menu selections have been made, and voted on by all family members (my wife, myself, and our two dogs, Herb, and Lovejoy), I can begin the process of planning out the week.

The same holds true for that huge dinner party. The Planning stage works for all meals, ultra big, or small. Here are some of the questions you will ask yourself during the Planning stage.

- **The meal**
    - What am I serving (from appetizer's to dessert, or soup to nuts)
- **Ingredients**
    - What do I have on hand (spices, etc) and **NEVER** assume
    - What do I need (make a list, and check it twice)
- **Equipment**
    - Do I have the necessary tools (pots, pans, etc)
    - If not, can I substitute (i.e. a blender for a food processor)
- **Skill**
    - Have I mastered the techniques necessary to create this recipe
    - If not, can I pull it off, or do I want to experiment on my friends

As you can see, if this is a simple week-night meal for your family, the entire planning process might only take five minutes...

## Bada Bing, Bada Boom.

# The Beginning of the Journey

## The Big Test

Let's give the plan a test and see how it works in a real-life situation that involves family, food, and fun (you didn't really expect to get out of this class without a test... did you). You're planning a Saturday event for your family and friends, and it's basically a retirement party for your next-door neighbor... this really happened.

## The Guest List

You've got a general idea of whose coming to the party, and it's 35 warm bodies, with people dropping in and out as the day progresses. We'll assume, for the moment, that it isn't going to rain (it could happen), so with that many bodies, this is going to be an outdoor party. You check the guest list, and it includes the very young and the rather old.

You can count on some people drinking, some not, and children who want all kinds of strange beverages. You also notice that some of the people are vegetarians. By 6:00pm the crowd settles down to 15 close friends and family, who will be staying for a causal outdoor dinner.

I've never thrown a party, or catered an event, without having a general knowledge of who's coming to dinner. As you can see it gives you a good idea on what you can serve and what you can't. Remember, as the host (and chef), it's not about what you want to eat, it's about what your guests want to eat.

The party kicks off around 1:00pm, and will continue into the evening. The general party will have folks coming and going, and will end at 6:pm. That's when the private dinner for the fifteen invited guests begins. You figure the last guest will exit around 10:00pm. In other words we're talking an all-day event.

Although there will be one main time that the 15 guests will eat (6:30pm), you're going to want to serve the other guests bits & bites as the day progresses, and you will need to provide some form of refreshment, and even a bit of entertainment.

As you can see, we already have a ton of information that we can use to plan this little party. Therefore, knowing who's on the list, gives a general idea of what you're going to serve, and gives you a general theme for the party... and that's the next step in planning.

# Step 1: Planning

## What to Eat

Okay, you've got vegetarians, and the normal variety carnivore. You could go both ways, and have some meat, fish, and plant dishes; however, you're the chef, and you have to make the hard decisions... you decide to go with fish and veggies.

We're building on the knowledge we've been given: 35 warm bodies, of various ages. Those dropping by in the early afternoon are just there to congratulate the retiree on making it this far, and they don't expect to be fed, so simple bite-size appetizers are all that's needed.

We'll need the recipes, some appetizers, drinks, and entertainment. From this information we come up with the following:

### General Refreshments: 1:00PM - 6:00PM

- **Appetizers**
  - Red & Green Bell Pepper Quiches
  - Crab Quiches
- **Refreshments**
  - White Wine
  - Raspberry Ice Tea
  - Assorted Soft Drinks

### Private Dinner: 6:30 - 8:00

- **Main Course**
  - Cedar Plank Grilled Atlantic Salmon (Oh Yeah, Baby)
- **Side Dishes**
  - Steamed Fresh Corn on the Cob
  - Rice Pilaf
- **Dessert**
  - Carrot Cake

# The Beginning of the Journey

## *Appitizers*

The quiches you're making require a crust, and you decide on a French *pate brisee*. It's a lite flaky crust. The dough can be made, and the quiche shells baked several days before the party, then frozen until needed. The average consumption of bite-size quiches is 6 to 8 per person. You will have some small children who might not eat as many; so you decide to do 5 per person. It's simple math: 5 x 35 = 175 quiche cups. A typical quiche baking pan (it's like a cupcake baking pan with smaller places for the quiche cups), will bake 24 cups at a time. You happen to have 2, which means you can bake 48 cups at a time, and that comes out to 4 baking sessions. It will take about 2 hours to prepare the quiche dough (including letting the dough rest in the refrigerator for an hour), and blind baking the cups takes 13 minutes. You have 4 baking sessions, or 52 minutes of total baking time (13 x 4). Add the two hours of prep time, and it will take you 2 hours and 52 minutes to pre-bake the cups. You decide to pre-bake the cups a day or two in advance. That doesn't mean that you're about to spend three hours in the kitchen. Most of that time is taken up with resting the dough, and baking. In addition, you will need to bake the cake, and you decide to that the day before the party.

You will also need to chop the peppers and onions into a small dice, and prepare a basic quiche custard. These steps need to be done the morning of the party, and will take about 1 hour.

The final step is the filling & baking of the quiches. You have 5 hours of random guests until the main party, so you decide to bake 35 quiches, set them out, and repeat that process every hour. The filling and baking of 35 quiches will take about 20 minutes. Most of that 20 minutes will be taken up in the oven. It will only take about 5 minutes of your time to actually fill the cups.

## *Refreshments*

This is an easy one. You will need 8 bottles of wine (you figure Chardonnay is a safe bet), a couple of six packs of assorted soft drinks for the kids, and 3 gallons of raspberry-flavored ice tea. The tea should be made the day before, and allowed to steep with the raspberries. The other drinks can be picked up, any time.

# Step 1: Planning

## The Meal

You're making Atlantic Salmon, planked on the grill for the private 15 quests. Your fish monger tells you that he has some excellent salmon coming in early on the morning of your party. The average serving of salmon would be from 1/3 to 1/2 pound per person. Since there are 15 guests invited to the private party, you check to see if you can get 2 salmon filets, about 4 pounds each... he says you can, so you order them. You'll pick them up the morning of the party, put them into a simple oil, lemon & pepper marinade, and then cook them on the grill in about 12 to 14 minutes.

Since you're going to the store to pick up the salmon, you decide to pick up the corn, rice, plus the crab and bell peppers for the quiches that same morning (fresh is best). For the corn, you'll need your large steamer pot, and water. The corn will take about 30 minutes. Knowing this lets you know when to put on the side dishes, so they'll be ready when the salmon is done.

The cake should be made the day before, and the quiche cups can be made a week early and frozen. Since you're going to the store earlier in the week, you pick up the materials you need for the quiche cups, and the cake and, while there, you go ahead and pick up the wine, tea, raspberries, and soft drinks.

Make a sweep around your kitchen see what you already have, and unless you have a perfect memory, develop a shopping list of all the needed items (spices, etc). This probably pegs me as a geek; however, I wrote a bit of a program that has all my recipes; when I select all the ones that I want to use, it will generate a shopping list of all the ingredients, separated into categories: Poultry, Meats, Veggies, etc... that's what I call being a geek.

Notice that we're not picking up, or doing anything yet. We're just getting a time line for the events. Once, you've established what you're going to get, stick it to your refrigerator. I've got one of those French chef pigs, holding a blackboard, and I write on that... whatever.

This first step is the most time-consuming of the six; however, with a bit a practice, it goes fairly fast. As a matter of fact, I only took me about twenty minutes of planning to come up with the information I needed to complete the other five steps.

# The Beginning of the Journey

# Step 2: Purchasing

## You get what you pay for

I used to hear that expression "Andy, you get what you pay for," in the broken English of my Aunt Josephine as we walked through the many farmer's markets dotted in and around the Chicago area. As we walked and talked, she would constantly be testing the farmer's wares with a thump and a sniff... I really miss those days.

Good ingredients can sometimes cost more; however, in many cases they will make the meal. For example, the conception of making a pot-luck stew by taking everything that you haven't used in the last week or two, throwing it all into a pot, adding some water, and turning on the heat is not right... Good luck with that one.

A good pot luck stew begins with good, fresh ingredients... enough said.

My aunt went shopping for the fresh ingredients for her recipes on a daily basis. If something lasted in the refrigerator for more than a few days, it was thrown out. However, since she planned her meals well, she seldom wasted any food.

The Plan you made in Step 1 will give you the list of all the ingredients needed to prepare your luscious meal, and help to keep your loss to a minimum.

- **What do you need in terms of ingredients**
    - Dry or canned ingredients can be purchased far in advance
    - Veggies should be purchased within 24 hours of the event
    - Make sure meats are fresh (get to know your butcher)
    - Fish should smell salty & fresh (like the ocean); avoid fish that smells fishy
    - Buy organic, if possible

The purchasing part of the plan is easy, because you have already created the shopping list in step 1... all you need to do now, is get in the car, and drive to the old grocery store.

# You Get What You Pay For

# Step 3: Prepping

## The work before the work

Prepping before the initial cooking begins is a smart thing to do. For example, if the recipe calls for a lot of chopping, slicing, and dicing, and other do-ahead stuff, it's not a bad idea to do some prepping.

By definition, a *Prep Chef* is responsible for preparing all of the ingredients for the *Line Chef*... do you really believe all those television chefs prepare their own ingredients?

If you can't afford a prep chef, then prepping the ingredients is left up to you, or possibly your guests (if they haven't had too much wine). For example, if the recipe calls for a cup of diced carrots, you can dice them ahead of time, or if you need a teaspoon each of oregano, thyme, and rosemary, why not measure those ingredients out ahead of time, place them into small bowls, and add them to the recipe as required... Just like those big-time television chefs. Prepping before a meal is optional, but it's a good thing to do.

The prepping of the meal is determined by the recipes that you are preparing, and the complexity of the ingredients that you are using.

For example, you create a mirepoix as a base for some soup. A mirepoix is basically diced onions, celery, and carrots, so you put a bit of olive oil into a pan, and begin to saute' the onions. Now it's time to add the carrots and celery; however, you never diced them... oops. This is an obvious example; however, the dicing of all the ingredients ahead of time is defined as prepping, and I promise you that it will save you a lot of frustration, once the cooking begins.

In our example menu, there are several things that you did ahead of time that would be defined as prepping. You pre-baked the quiche shells for the bell pepper, and the crab quiches. You made the carrot cake a day ahead of time. Finally, you made purchases of goods needed to make the meal... all ahead of time. By definition, that's prepping.

On the day of the meal, you can prep several items. For example, you can shuck the corn... that's easy. In addition, you could mix the oil, spices, and lemon juice used in the salmon marinade, and then store until needed.

# The Work Before the Work

Not only does prepping gives you greater control over the creation of the meal; in addition, you now have more time to visit with your guests, family and friends. And as previously mentioned, you could make the creation of the meal a group affair, by letting your guests help in the preparation.

On more than one occasion, I've had more guests in the kitchen with me, chopping, slicing, and dicing, than are outside by the pond or playing croquet. Give it a try...

## Tools of the trade

To do good prepping you will need: places to store your prepped ingredients until needed (refrigerator, counter top), and prep storage (bowls, cups, whatever). For example, most chefs have dozens of small, medium, and large prep bowls. Stores like Williams-Sonoma and Bed Bath & Beyond are excellent places to find everything that you'll need to get the job done. Oh, and don't forget the cling wrap to place over the top of the bowls.

# Step 4: Preparing

## The moment of truth

In my opinion, this is where the fun starts. It's your time to perform. You've made all the plans, purchased all the ingredients, and even prepped the ingredients. It's time to do your thing. You step confidently into the kitchen, tie on that apron that says: Kiss the Chef (a present from my wife), and go for it.

- Clean and set up the kitchen work areas
- Know where everything is in your kitchen
    - Use a time chart (on paper, or in your head) to keep everything in order
    - Have fun

Are you winging it? I should say not... It's all part of the plan... that marvellous, wonderful plan.

## The time line

A time line is a sequence of steps, and when you need to perform them. For example (and this is an easy one), if you have to bake potatoes for 90 minutes, and steam some corn (30 minutes)... and you want them both to come out at the same time, you would start the potatoes 60 minutes before you start the corn... See, I said that was an easy one.

If you cook professionally, most time lines are in the chef's head. They've been burned into their brains, by doing the recipe over, and over, and over again, until it almost becomes a habit.

A time line, or a flowchart of events, can look like it was designed by an accountant, or it can be as simple as jotting down a few starting times on a piece of paper.

# The Moment Of Truth

## Kitchen Planner

Date: _____  Event: _____  Dine Time: _____

Notes: _____

| Time    |   | Task                        |
|---------|---|-----------------------------|
| 8:00am  | - | Pick up salmon              |
| 9:15am  | - | Place salmon into marinade  |
| 12:00pm | - | Set up dinning area         |
| 12:30pm | - | Make first set of quiches   |
| 1:30pm  | - | Make second set of quiches  |
| . . . . . . . . . . . . . . . |   |                             |

# Step 5: Plating

## Bring out that hidden artist in you

Plating and Presenting go hand-in-hand because they're both the visual side of the meal. Remember this: We eat first with our eyes. Smell, taste, and mouth feel come next, but our first contact with food is with our eyes (depending on the direction of the wind).

That's not to say that well-presented food doesn't taste bad, or that poorly presented food doesn't taste good; however, we make our first decision on whether we will like or dislike a particular dish by what we see.

Have some fun here. For example, you could use plain French white plates, and decorate them with a sprinkle of dry herbs, or you could have a couple of squeeze bottles containing different color sauces (we'll talk more about that later), and paint designs on the plates.

- Plate with color... color is a strong visual motivator.
- Plating dishes is an art form
- Work with different colors to create artistic dishes

# Making It Look Delicious

# Step 6: Presenting

## The moment of truth

Plating is accomplished in the kitchen, Presenting is accomplished at the table, or wherever you're planning on serving your meal. This is the moment of truth. This is when everything comes together. Presentation is all about tablecloths, decorations, and all the little details that make a meal fun; even the smile on your face as you deliver the meal to the table is a part of the presentation.

When you bring the food to the guests, four things begin to happen:

- **Visual**: We eat first with our eyes... Well-plated dishes produce a great visual effect.
- **Smell**: Smells work with our brain (food memories), and actually helps us to taste our food.
- **Taste**: Create layers of flavor in your dishes.
- **Mouth Feel**: One bite crunchy, one bite smooth... I can't wait for the next bite.

## Summary

While using six steps to prepare a meal may seem a bit much, in reality the process becomes quite simple with practice. Success in a kitchen requires a bit of organizational skill, and even if you don't consider yourself an organized person this book will literally change how you view cooking.

I promise that if you use these six steps in your meal preparation, you will first gain *Control* over the kitchen, and *Control* leads to *Confidence*, and finally *Control* and *Confidence* in the kitchen lead to *Creativity*.

Confidence, Control, and Creativity: the secret to culinary success, great meals, and happy family and friends are only a few steps away. Who could ask for anything more?

# The Big Event

## *In Conclusion*

Planning is the most crucial step in the process, and it's the step that gives you the information to complete the other five steps. The good news is that once you've mastered the art of planning, it becomes easier and easier.

Think of the planning stage as being the conductor of an orchestra, the musicians are your tools to get the job done, and the musical score is your menu. You boldly step up to the podium, raise your baton, and the music begins to fill the auditorium. If you're in control, the music is fantastic; however, if you didn't do your homework, it might go a bit sour.

Planning is your homework, and it involves everything from organizational skills, to mastery of cooking.

So do your homework well…

# Eggs & Such

Breakfast is considered by many to be the most important meal of the day. The word literally means the breaking of a fast. It is the first meal consumed after dinner and a night's sleep; which could be 8 hours or more (assuming you didn't do any late-night snacking).

Breakfasts can consist of a piece of toast on the run, a total fry up, or some compromise in-between. Ham, sausages, eggs; as well as, pancakes and waffles are all fair game when it come to the day's first meal.

Roman soldiers woke up to a breakfast of pulmentus, a porridge similar to the Italian polenta, made from roasted spelt wheat or barley that was then pounded and cooked in a cauldron of water. On the march, they ate bucellatum, dried bread similar to Holland rusk. People in the Middle East made and grilled flatbreads of all kinds, perhaps accompanied by green onions or another easily cultivated vegetable and a soft cheese, a tradition that carries through to the present time.

By Victorian times, when abundance was enjoyed by Americans as well as the British at the height of the British Empire, breakfast was a lavish affair, whether served at a table in a farm kitchen or in an elegant city dining room. Cookbooks from the period provide insight into the breakfast served by affluent households. In the 1861 Book of Household Management, Isabella Beeton suggested a daily breakfast buffet that included a cold joint of meat, game pies, broiled mackerel, sausages, bacon and eggs, muffins, toast, marmalade, butter, jam, coffee, and tea (now that's what I call a breakfast).

Here in the United States we enjoy other types of breakfast foods, some more healthy than others. In addition to fruit juices, particularly orange juice, pancakes, biscuits, eggs, bacon, sausages, and other breakfast meats, we also consume hash brown potatoes and breakfast pastries such as coffee cakes, donuts, and muffins. About 7 percent of Americans enjoy a Southern-style breakfast with eggs, sausage, grits, and biscuits. On-the-go breakfasters—now about 68 percent of the population— might stop at a fast-food restaurant for a cup of coffee, a breakfast sandwich, a bagel, or a doughnut. Fast-food restaurants have expanded their breakfast offerings while the number of bagel emporiums and coffee shops has greatly increased to meet the growing needs of these breakfasters on the way to work or school. Health-conscious eaters favor breakfast cereal bars, plain bagels, yogurt, and herbal tea or fresh-squeezed carrot juice, and have prompted this segment of the prepared foods market to burgeon. About 32 percent of Americans currently eat toast for breakfast (now that's just plain sad).

# Unique Ideas for Breakfast and more

*breakfast*     Plan · Purchase · Prep · Prepare · Plate · Present

# Fantastic French Toast

To me, French toast is all about a crispy exterior with a soft, almost custard-like interior (let's not forget flavor), dipped and cooked in a whipped egg mixture. The egg might be an essential ingredient; however, it should not overpower the gentle sweetness that characterizes great French toast.

French toast, or pain perdu (lost bread), was the way for the practical French to salvage old bread. They would dip it in a simple egg batter and fry it; traditionally, in an iron skillet.

## Plan/Purchase

### Ingredients

| | |
|---|---|
| 1 | large egg |
| 2 | T. unsalted butter melted, plus extra for frying |
| 3/4 | c. milk |
| 2 | t. vanilla extract |
| 2 | T. granulated sugar |
| 1/3 | c. unbleached all-purpose flour |
| 1/4 | t. salt |
| 4–5 | slices day-old dense bread (3/4-inch-thick) or day-old sandwich bread |

### Did You Know

Although usually served as a sweetly spiced dish in the United States, some prefer a savory version, seasoned with salt and pepper instead, as is more common in the United Kingdom.

You just gotta love those Brits...

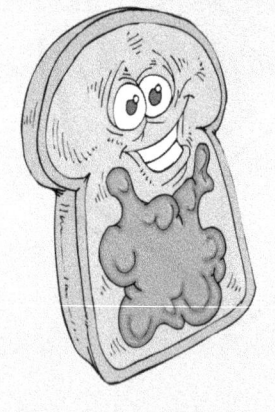

## Prep/Prepare

1. Heat a large skillet (cast-iron, if you have one) over medium heat for 5 minutes.
2. Lightly beat egg in shallow pan; then whisk in butter, milk, & vanilla.
3. Whisk in sugar, flour, & salt, until the mixture takes on a smooth consistency.
4. Add a bread slice, and soak for about 30 seconds per side (don't over soak). Remove bread & allow excess batter to drip back into the pan; repeat with remaining slices.
5. Add 1-tablespoon butter to hot skillet. Transfer prepared bread to skillet & cook until golden brown, about 1.5 minutes, flip & cook the second side for about 1 minute.

**Note: If cooking more, use an additional tablespoon of butter for each new batch.**

## Plate/Present

French toast should be plated and served fresh from the pan.

Though thick-sliced dense bread is best, you could use a high quality, pre sliced sandwich bread (make sure the slices are about 3/4 of an inch thick).

Flipping the bread can be accomplished with tongs (okay), or a spatula (best). And, if you're feeling romantic, you might just cut the toast into heart shapes before frying (just a suggestion).

You might even vary the flavor of the batter by adding a bit of ground cinnamon or nutmeg. You could even try replacing the vanilla with almond extract.

Additions are the obvious: powdered sugar, maple syrup, and some fruit. However, some prefer to forgo the additions, and simply enjoy the treat without extras. Other additions, might be some whipped cream (decadent), or possibly a nice homemade Summer jam.

You should pre-warm your syrup before serving... this will keep everything nice and toasty hot.

*Cooking with a Plan Vol 1: Back to the Kitchen* — breakfast

# Sausage/Egg Casserole Surprise

*Alright, I'll admit it... there is no surprise (that's the surprise), unless you consider a breakfast recipe, simply bursting with great flavor a surprise.*

*Reserve it for those occasions when you have the time to prepare the ingredients the day before.*

*The mustard powder helps to balance the flavors of the pork sausage with the eggs and cheese, and ties the whole dish together, so don't leave it out.*

## Prep/Prepare

1. Crumble the sausage, & cook over medium heat until evenly browned.
2. Drain the sausage on paper towels to remove any excess grease.
3. Mix the mustard powder, salt, eggs & milk in a bowl
4. Add the sausage, bread cubes, & cheese, and gently stir to incorporate.
5. Pour mixture into a greased 9x13 inch baking dish, or ceramic baking bowl.
6. Let cool overnight in the refrigerator (cover with cling foil, to keep the casserole from absorbing any frig odors).
7. Preheat oven to 350° F.
8. Cover with foil, and bake 45 to 60 minutes.
9. Uncover, & reduce temperature to 325° F.
10. Bake an additional 30 minutes, or until eggs are firmly set.

## Plate/Present

In our home, breakfasts have a tendency to be more on the casual side of the fence. As a matter of fact, it's not unusual to see most of my guests sitting at the table in their PJ's, hair uncombed, and no makeup... not a pretty site, but a homey one.

A dish like this is perfect for a casual morning. Serve it in the baking dish, and let everyone scoop out their own portions. Oh, and don't forget tea, coffee, and a bit of juice.

And since this is served right out of the oven, make sure your guests know that the serving dish is hot, hot, hot.

A more elegant way to serve this dish would be to prepare and cook, using individual ramekins.

While the dish does contain bread, I like to serve this dish with mouth watering buttermilk biscuits using the recipe on page 52... Yummy.

## Plan/Purchase

### Ingredients

| | |
|---|---|
| 1 | lb. ground pork sausage |
| 1 | t. mustard powder |
| 1/2 | t. salt |
| 6 | eggs, beaten |
| 2 | c. milk |
| 6 | slices white bread, toasted and cut into cubes |
| 8 | oz. sharp Cheddar cheese, shredded |
| - | fresh ground black pepper, and salt, to taste |

### What the recipe doesn't know

*How far ahead you're preparing this dish...* The pre-planning on this dish is not just important, it's essential, because the time in the refrigerator gives the ingredients time to meld, and get to know each other.

~ 49 ~

*breakfast*  Plan · Purchase · Prep · Prepare · Plate · Present

# Southwest Eggs & Chili with cheese

Scrambled eggs are traditionally thought of as something consumed at breakfast; while chili is more of a lunch or dinner item. This recipe combines the heartiness of chili with the delicate taste and texture of fresh scrambled eggs, for an any-time-you-want-it dish.

Can you serve it for breakfast... of course you can. Can you serve it for dinner... go for it. You pick the time, you pick the place; however, I guarantee that whenever you eat this dish will be the right time.

## Plan/Purchase

### Ingredients

| | |
|---|---|
| 16 | eggs |
| 1/4 | c. half & half |
| 1 | t. salt, plus more, to taste |
| - | Freshly ground pepper, to taste |
| 3 | T. canola oil |
| 1 | yellow onion, diced |
| 5 | oz. sharp cheddar cheese, shredded |
| 4 1/2 | c. beef and bean chili |

### Tip

*If you're not a great fan of canned chili (I'm not), then use the chili recipe on page 134 to really kick up the taste of this dish. You'll love it.*

### Technique

*Check out the method for cooking scrambled eggs on page 58. It's a great way to keep the eggs fluffy and creamy.*

### What the recipe doesn't know

**When you made the chili...** *there are all kinds of chili, and all kinds of chili lovers. Choose a chili to you and your guests liking, and since chili can benefit from time spent in the frig, make the chili the day before and reheat when making the eggs.*

## Prep/Prepare

1. Prepare your chili in a pot & keep warm.
2. In a large bowl, whisk the eggs until combined.
3. Whisk in the half & half, with 1 t. salt and pepper.
4. Set a skillet over medium-high heat, & add the oil.
5. Add the onion, season with salt & pepper and then cook, stirring, for about 5 minutes, until the onions are translucent.
6. Pour in the egg mixture & stir with a spatula, making large curds, until the eggs are almost cooked through, 5 to 7 minutes.
7. Sprinkle with the cheese & stir until melted.

## Plate/Present

This is the kind of dish that is best prepared for each guest.

Use pre-warmed plates, if you can (see Techniques: Pre-Warming), because it will help to maintain the heat of the dish.

Place a generous portion of the eggs in the middle of the plate, and then ladle some of the warm chili over the top... not too much, or you will overpower the eggs.

If you're feeling artistic, drizzle some of the sauce around the eggs (hopefully your guests will be awake enough to appreciate your creative efforts), and then surround the mound of eggs and chili with four toast points (like the four points of a compass).

Coffee and juice for the morning, or ice tea, and maybe a glass of wine, if serving in the evening.

Serve immediately.

Cooking with a Plan Vol 1: Back to the Kitchen        breakfast

# Awesome Breakfast Burritos

*This is a great way to start the day with a surge of great flavor... just add your favorite salsa to this breakfast delight, and you'll wonder why you didn't fix it sooner.*

*Another advantage to this breakfast is that it's portable. Just open it up, add the salsa, and eat it on the run. Just be careful, you don't want to drip that salsa on your nice clean business outfit.*

*This is a traditional Mexican staple, and I guarantee that it will keep you happy though a hard day's work, all the way up to lunch.*

## Prep/Prepare

1. Dice the bacon, & then cook over medium high heat until brown. Drain, and set aside.
2. Wrap the tortillas in a damp cloth & warm in the oven.
3. In a small sauce pan heat the refried beans.
4. Fry the eggs in a greased skillet until the whites are firm & the yokes are cooked but still a bit runny.
5. Top each tortilla with refried beans, diced bacon (equal to two slices), 1 egg and a bit of cheese.
6. Roll tortillas into burritos & serve immediately.

## Plate/Present

Be casual here... Serve simply on a plate with the salsa on the side. You might want to add a slice or two of freshly cut apple or orange for an editable decoration.

## Let Yourself Go

How adventurous are you?

The eggs and bacon are only the beginning of a great adventure. How about sauteing some diced peppers, onions, and celery (just for starters), and rolling them in with the eggs. As a matter of fact, you'd be surprised what some diced apple would do to this dish.

In other words, have a bit of fun.

## For Your Information

The word burrito literally means "little donkey" in Spanish (Oh yeah, like you didn't already know that).

Here's something you might not know:

A United States court established that a burrito can not be defined as a sandwich...

Apparently the United States court system has too much time on their hands.

## Plan/Purchase

### Ingredients

| | |
|---|---|
| 1 | lb. bacon |
| 10 | eggs |
| 16 | oz. refried beans (1 can) |
| 8 | oz. shredded Cheddar cheese |
| 10 | flour tortillas (10 inch) |

### Additions

- Diced Bell Peppers
- Diced onion
- Diced celery
- Diced apple

You get the picture... if it's a veggie or fruit, and it can be diced, give it a try.

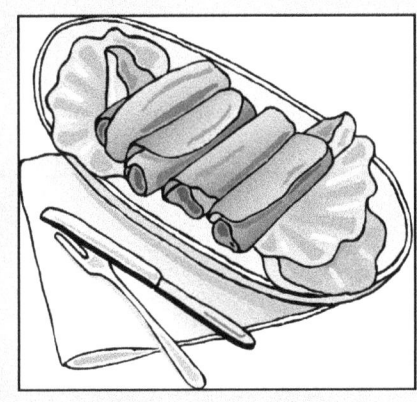

~ 51 ~

*breakfast*  Plan · Purchase · Prep · Prepare · Plate · Present

# Awesome Buttermilk Biscuits

*Fluffy buttermilk biscuits are the best... If you've never tasted one of these golden delights, then you're in for a treat a fantastic treat.*

*This recipe partially comes from my time spent studying in Tennessee, and partially from experimentation. Since I choose to freeze my butter, a good food processor fitted with a standard S-blade is the only way you're going to get that butter mixed into the flour. If you don't own a food processor, then just put the butter in the refrigerator.*

## Plan/Purchase

### Ingredients

| | | |
|---|---|---|
| 1 | c. | all-purpose flour |
| 1 | c. | cake flour (plain) |
| 2 | t. | baking powder |
| 1/2 | t. | baking soda |
| 1 | t. | sugar |
| 1/2 | t. | salt |
| 1/4 | lb. | unsalted butter (cut into 1/4 cubes and frozen) |
| 3/4 | c. | buttermilk (40° f) |
| 2 | T. | unsalted butter (melted) for brushing before baking |

### Baker's Tip

*As with all baking, oven temperature is a critical factor. A calibrated oven lets you know that you have the exact temperature, and for a stable environment, you should preheat the oven for 20 to 30 minutes before popping in the biscuits.*

## Prep/Prepare

1. Mix both flours (cake and all-purpose), with the baking powder, baking soda, sugar, & salt in the bowl of a food processor, fitted with an S blade.

2. Drop the frozen butter into the bowl, making sure that all the pieces are coated with the flour (the butter should be completely frozen: 20 to 30 minutes in the freezer).

3. Set the food processor to high speed and quick pulse (5 or 6, 1-second pulses). The butter/flour mixture should resemble course meal (all the butter is broken down & incorporated into the flour mixture, but there should still be some larger lumps). Do not over mix.

4. Reduce the speed on the blender to its lowest setting, & slowly drizzle the buttermilk into the flour mixture (remember to keep the buttermilk cold).

5. Continue to blend until the mixture pulls together into a soft ball (15 or 20 seconds). Do not over mix.

6. Remove the mixture from the bowl onto a lightly-floured surface, & form a ball.

7. Use a pastry scraper, or knife to cut the ball in half.

8. Form into balls, and wrap in plastic wrap.

9. Let the dough rest in the refrigerator for at least 1 hour.

10. Remove one of the dough balls from the refrigerator, unwrap, & place on a lightly-floured surface.

11. Using your hands, lightly press the dough into a pie shape about 6 inches in diameter (the dough should be about 1/2 inch thick).

12. Use a knife or pastry scraper to cut the dough into six equal pie shapes.

13. Form rough balls from each pie-shaped section.

14. Place the dough onto an ungreased cookie sheet, & brush the tops with the melted butter (or milk).

15. Place in a preheated 450° f. oven, until the tops of the biscuits are lightly browned (10 to 14 minutes).

Cooking with a Plan Vol I: Back to the Kitchen — breakfast

# Homemade Breakfast Sausage

*Of course we all know that you can purchase any number of breakfast sausages from your local grocer; however, making your own is not that difficult, and it gives you the ability to mix the spices into the sausage in exactly the right proportion for your individual taste.*

*Who knows, after some experimenting, you just might create the ultimate breakfast sausage. Just remember to keep the recipe in a safe place.*

## Prep/Prepare

1. In a small, bowl, combine the sage, salt, ground black pepper, marjoram, brown sugar, crushed red pepper & cloves.
2. Place the pork in a bowl and add the mixed spices.
3. Mix & form into patties.
4. Saute the patties in a large skillet over medium high heat for 5 minutes per side, or until internal pork temperature reaches 160° f.

## What the recipe doesn't know

**The type of sausage your using...** For example, you might not be a big fan of pork, so you could substitute low-fat turkey, or chicken... why not?

## Chef's Tip

Fresh sausage will keep for 5 days in the refrigerator, or you could slice the sausage into patties, freeze, and then remove and cook as many as you need. In the freezer, they should last (tightly covered) for two months.

## Plan/Purchase

### Ingredients

| | |
|---|---|
| 2 | t. dried sage |
| 2 | t. salt |
| 1 | t. ground black pepper |
| 1/4 | t. dried marjoram |
| 1 | T. brown sugar |
| 1/8 | t. crushed red pepper flakes |
| 1/8 | t. ground cloves |
| 2 | lb. ground pork |

### For Your Information

*Some people like to pour ketchup or other condiments onto their breakfast sausages; for instance, in some parts of the United States and Canada, it is routine to put maple syrup on breakfast sausages (that's what I do).*

### Chef's Note

*This particular version is one that I've put together over the course of time, and always has my overnight guests asking for more... give it a try.*

~ 53 ~

*breakfast* — Plan · Purchase · Prep · Prepare · Plate · Present

# Made From Scratch Granola

*I love going to Taos, New Mexico and spending a few days working on my Tex Mex recipes. There's this particular bed & breakfast, right in the middle of town, that serves the best homemade granola I've ever tasted. The hotel keeps it a closely guarded secret, and even the hotel staff doesn't know the recipe.*

*After many trials, I came up with what I believe to be a close representation of that wonderful breakfast dish. If you like granola, I promise that you'll love this mixture.*

## Plan/Purchase

### Ingredients

| | | |
|---|---|---|
| 8 | c. | rolled oats |
| 1 1/2 | c. | wheat germ |
| 1 1/2 | c. | oat bran |
| 1 | c. | sunflower seeds |
| 1 | c. | finely chopped almonds |
| 1 | c. | finely chopped pecans |
| 1 | c. | finely chopped walnuts |
| 1 1/2 | t. | salt |
| 1/2 | c. | brown sugar |
| 1/4 | c. | maple syrup |
| 3/4 | c. | honey |
| 1 | c. | vegetable oil |
| 1 | t. | ground cinnamon |
| 1 | t. | vanilla extract |
| 2 | c. | raisins or sweetened dried cranberries |

### Chef's Tip

This is the kind of recipe that begs experimentation. For example, you could pick up some dried fruit, and add them to the mix. Or substitute honey for the maple syrup.

It's totally up to you, and your culinary imagination.

## Prep/Prepare

1. Preheat the oven to 325° f.
2. Line two large baking sheets with parchment (personally, I'm not a big fan of baking with aluminum foil).
3. Combine the oats, wheat germ, oat bran, sunflower seeds, almonds, pecans, & walnuts in a large bowl.
4. Stir together the salt, brown sugar, maple syrup, honey, oil, cinnamon, & vanilla in a saucepan. Bring to a boil over medium heat, pour over the dry ingredients, & stir to coat.
5. Spread the mixture evenly on the baking sheets.
6. Bake in the preheated oven until crispy and toasted, about 20 minutes. Stir once halfway through.
7. Cool, then stir in the raisins or cranberries before storing in an airtight container.

## Plate/Present

Serve in a large bowl with smaller bowls for your guests. Some good vanilla yogurt goes good, as well as some fresh fruit (strawberries, apples, peaches, etc).

Go for it...

# A Proper British Breakfast

*"This is a traditional breakfast in Britain, or at least as I remember it. The British refer to it as a "fry up". It might not be the type of breakfast you would serve everyday; however, it's fun to experiment with other cultures and their interpretation of the first meal of the day.*

*The egg can be scrambled (if you like), and if you're feeling real British, you might even want to add some black pudding.*

## Prep/Prepare

1. Heat the oil in a skillet over medium heat. Add the sausage & hash browns. Fry until browned on one side, about 5 minutes. Turn them over to fry on the other side & add the tomato, bacon & mushrooms. The idea is to start cooking with the things that take the longest.
2. When just about cooked, crack the egg into the center & allow to cook. You might want to add a little more oil just to crisp the edges. Toast the slice of bread while the egg cooks & then spread butter on it. Serve everything on a plate with the toast on the side.

## Did You Know

Black pudding or blood pudding is a sausage made by cooking animal blood with a filler until it is thick enough to congeal when cooled. I don't know about you, but that's too much information.

## Plan/Purchase

### Ingredients

| | |
|---|---|
| 1/4 | c. vegetable oil |
| 1 | link pork sausage |
| 1 | frozen hash brown patty |
| 2 | thick slices bacon |
| 1 | tomato, cut in half |
| 4 | mushrooms, sliced |
| 1 | egg |
| 1 | slice white bread |
| 1 | t. butter |

### Did You Know

A British breakfast can consist of hot cutlets, pink hams, fried soles, devilled kidneys, little crisp rolls of bacon, dishes of scrambled eggs and sausages, black pudding, a cold grouse or pheasant, a piece of pie and then hot toast in white napkins, fresh rolls, sweet butter, marmalades of all colors, jams, jellies and pyramids of fruit. Now that's what I call a breakfast.

### Chef's Tip

I wouldn't recommend eating a breakfast like this every day... still, it's a pretty good way to start the morning.

~ 55 ~

*breakfast*   Plan · Purchase · Prep · Prepare · Plate · Present

# To Die For Waffles

*This recipe is about as simple as it gets; however, don't let that fool you. The waffles are crispy on the inside with a soft interior, and the vanilla helps to bring together all of the flavors.*

*The honeycombed surface of this crisp, light bread is perfect for holding pockets of your favorite syrup. There are a number of waffle-iron shapes available including square, rectangular, round and even heart-shape. Just make sure that you have a lot of batter, because I promise you that your family and guests will be asking for more... and more... and more.*

## Plan/Purchase

### Ingredients

| | |
|---|---|
| 2 | c. all-purpose flour |
| 1 | t. salt |
| 4 | t. baking powder |
| 2 | T. white sugar |
| 2 | eggs |
| 1 1/2 | c. warm milk |
| 1/3 | c. butter, melted |
| 1 | t. vanilla extract |

### Cooking Tip

*I recommend an electric mixer or immersion blender to do the blending. That way the ingredients will be smooth without any unwanted lumps...*

*I hate it when I get lumps.*

### Chef's Tip

*Don't forget to pre-heat the syrup. You don't want to go pouring cold syrup on hot waffles... or do you?*

~ 56 ~

## Prep/Prepare

1. In a large bowl, mix together flour, salt, baking powder & sugar; set aside.
2. In a separate bowl, beat the eggs. Stir in the milk, butter & vanilla. Pour the milk mixture into the flour mixture; beat until blended.
3. Ladle the batter into a preheated waffle iron. Cook the waffles until golden & crisp. Serve immediately.

## Did You Know

Belgian waffles, are often heaped with fresh strawberries and whipped cream. Oh Yeah Baby!!!

Cooking with a Plan Vol 1: Back to the Kitchen     breakfast

# Unique Baked Omelet with gooey cheese

Here's my interesting twist on the traditional omelet-in-a-pan recipe. In this case all the cooking is done in the oven, so there's no mess on the stove top.

A traditional omelet consists of a mixture of eggs, seasonings and sometimes water or milk, cooked in butter and filled or topped with various fillings such as cheese, ham, mushrooms, onions, peppers, sausage and herbs. This recipe carries on the tradition... but with a few little twists, and when you serve this breakfast to your guests, it's sure to open a few eyes.

## Prep/Prepare

1. Preheat oven to 450° f.
2. Lightly grease a 9x13 inch baking pan.
3. In a blender, combine eggs, milk, flour, salt & pepper; cover & process until smooth.
4. Pour into prepared baking pan. Spread until it totally covers the bottom of the pan.
5. Bake in preheated oven until set, about 20 minutes.
6. Remove from oven, and sprinkle with cheese.
7. Carefully loosen edges of omelet from pan. Starting from the short edge of the pan, roll up the omelet.

## Plate/Present

Place omelet seam side down on a serving plate and cut into 6 equal sized pieces.

Sprinkle some grated cheese on top, and serve immediately.

The recipe goes well with the buttermilk biscuits located on page 52.

## Chef's Tip

If you make your omelets using the traditional pan method. The high heat can cause your butter to brown, thus imparting a unwanted nutty flavor to the dish.

You can solve this by using clarified butter. See Appendix A: Techniques, for instructions on making clarified butter.

## Plan/Purchase

### Ingredients

| | |
|---|---|
| 6 | eggs |
| 1 | c. milk |
| 1/2 | c. all-purpose flour |
| 1/2 | t. salt |
| 1/4 | t. ground black pepper |
| 1 | c. shredded Cheddar cheese |

### Tasty Addidtions

This recipe is easy to personalize. For example, you could put some crumbled bacon into the roll, or even some of your favorite veggies.

Like any recipe, have some fun and experiment a bit.

### Did You Know

A Western omelette, also known as a Denver omelette, is an omelette sometimes filled with diced ham, onions, and green bell peppers.

But maybe you already knew that.

breakfast     Plan · Purchase · Prep · Prepare · Plate · Present

# Creamy Scrambled Eggs

If you think that scrambled eggs are all equal, then you've never tasted good scrambled eggs. The ingredients are simple; however, it's the cooking technique used, that will make the difference between creamy eggs, and dried scrambled bits.

Properly made scrambled eggs should be moist in texture with a creamy consistency and delicate flavor. Try this recipe, and you'll have perfect scrambled eggs every time.

## Plan/Purchase

### Ingredients

| | |
|---|---|
| 2 | eggs |
| 2 | t. cream |
| 1 | t. water (optional) |
| 1 | t. butter |
| - | salt and pepper to taste (optional) |

### Cooking Tip

Remember to cook the eggs slowly over low heat, and push to center. Then tilt the pan to allow the runny parts to go to the sides, and push to center.

### Food Tip

The residual heat within the eggs will keep them cooking after they are removed from the pan. If you wait until they are fully cooked before removing them from the pan, they will most likely be too dry, when served.

### Chef's Tip

An easy way to tell fresh eggs is look to see if the white of the eggs is firm. When eggs get old and some of the proteins break down, the whites will begin to go runny.

## Prep/Prepare

1. In a cup or small bowl, whisk together the eggs, cream & water using a fork.
2. Melt butter in a skillet over low heat.
3. Add whisked eggs to pan.
4. Do not stir immediately. Wait until the first hint of setting begins.
5. Using a spatula or flat wooden spoon, gently push the eggs to the center of the pan, & then tilt the skillet to distribute runny parts to the edges.
6. Continue this technique as the eggs continue to set.
7. After a time, the eggs will be set, with no runny parts.
8. Flip the eggs over, and cook 15 to 25 seconds longer.

## Plate/Present

Scrambled eggs are typically served with other items, such as toast, or breakfast meats. In addition, they can be presented in small hollowed-out Brioche or tartlets.

## Did You Know

If any liquid is seeping from the eggs, this is a sign of overcooking, or adding under cooked high-moisture vegetables.

## For Your Information

Scrambled egg products are available in various forms for use at home. Different products available include: Liquid Whole Eggs, Liquid Egg Substitute, Powdered Whole Eggs, Powdered Egg Substitute, Frozen Egg Products, and others.

# Appetizers

Dishes served before a meal or at a cocktail party or other informal occasion are often referred to as snacks or hors d' oeuvres. If there is a long waiting period between when the guests arrive and when the meal is served, these might serve the purpose of sustaining guests during the long wait.

Technically, any small, bite-size food served before a meal to whet and excite the palate could be defined as an appetizer; however, the term hors d' oeuvres, more correctly describes finger food, whereas appetizers can also apply to a first course served at the table.

Hors d' oeuvres should include light foods that may be cold or hot, but perhaps the most important feature of the dish is that it should be decorative in order to stimulate the appetite.

In French, Hors d' oeuvres refers to the food served before or outside of (French: hors) the main dishes of a meal (oeuvre).

Whatever you call them, they are an excellent way to kick off a great dinner party, excite your guests, whet their appetites, and get them ready for the main event.

Depending on the size of the hors d' oeuvres, and the amount of time until the main meal, a general rule of thumb is to have 6 to 8 per person. That's assuming that the size of the hors d' oeuvre is about one bite. If they are larger; adjust accordingly. You don't want to fill your guests up before the main meal.

Traditionally, hors d' oeuvres are served with glasses of wine, or whatever beverage you choose.

It's been said that if you get your guests drunk enough before they eat, they will always love your food.

I've hosted more than one party where I can attest to the accuracy of the above statement...

# (hors d' oeuvres) Off to a Good Start

*starter*  Plan · Purchase · Prep · Prepare · Plate · Present

# Crusted Goat Cheese Medallions

*The purpose of the hors d'œuvre (or what I call the starter) is to whet the appetite; if there is a long waiting period between when the guests arrive and when the meal is served (for example, during a cocktail hour), these might also serve the purpose of sustaining guests during the long wait.*

*These little bite size babies are chock full of flavor, and give your guests just enough to hold them over until the serving of the main course. In addition, they could be used as a salad to accompany the main meal.*

## Plan/Purchase

### Tomato Salsa

| | |
|---|---|
| 1/2 | c. tomatoes, chopped |
| 1/4 | c. shallots, minced |
| 1/4 | c. chopped fresh parsley |
| 2 | T. olive oil |
| 2 | T. red wine vinegar |
| 2 | T. fresh oregano, minced |
| - | Salt/Pepper, to taste |

### Goat Cheese

| | |
|---|---|
| 1/3 | c. bread crumbs |
| 1/3 | c. slivered almonds |
| 8 | oz. soft goat cheese |
| 1 | egg, beaten |
| 1 | T. olive oil |

### Spinach

| | |
|---|---|
| 8 | c. fresh spinach |
| 1/4 | t. red pepper flakes |
| 1/4 | t. kosher salt |

### Spinach

*A plant with dark green spear-shaped leaves. Spinach has a slightly bitter flavor. It is high in nutritional content and can be eaten raw or cooked.*

### Bread Crumbs

*It's best to make fresh bread crumbs for this recipe, and avoid, (if you can) the dried out crumbs-in-a-can.*

*If you must use store-bought crumbs try to find Japanese Panco bread crumbs... they're the best.*

## Prep/Prepare

1. Combine the ingredients for the salsa in a small bowl. Season with salt & pepper, cover and chill.
2. Pulse bread crumbs and almonds together in a food processor until fine.
3. Slice cheese into eight 1/2-inch slices. Dip each slice into the egg, then coat with the almond mixture.
4. Brown coated cheese in 1T oil in a nonstick skillet over medium heat (20-30 seconds, each side). Drain medallions on paper towels; return pan to the burner.
5. Sauté spinach with pepper flakes & salt until wilted, about 1 minute.

## Did You Know

8 cups of spinach might seem like a lot; however, it will wilt down quickly. Add about half the spinach to the pan, and let it wilt, then add the rest until fully wilted.

## Plate/Present

On a small plate, place a bed of wilted spinach, put two goat cheese bites in the middle, and then top with a spoonful or two of the tomato salsa. Garnish with a sprig of fresh parsley.

They should still be slightly warm... **YUMMY!**

## What the recipe doesn't know

**The type of goat cheese that you're using.** Typically, goat cheese is soft, fresh, unpressed and uncooked cheese made from goat's milk. It's also known as chévre. It comes plain, or mixed with spices, such as pepper (my favorite).

For this recipe, the goat cheese needs to be in a roll about 1.5 inches thick, and 4 inches long. This will allow you to make eight 1/2-inch medallions.

~ 62 ~

Cooking with a Plan Vol I: Back to the Kitchen    starter

# Baked Green Olives & Cheese

*Here's a bit size bit of flavor that's easy to make and great to eat.*

*It's also fun, because since the olives are actually wrapped and baked, your guests won't know what they're eating until they bite into one. With that in mind, I call them little olive surprises.*

*Although the recipe calls for green olives, you can try just about anything that you like. Just make sure that the pits have been removed, or one of your guests just might crack a tooth.*

## Prep/Prepare

1. Cream the room temperature butter in a large bowl. Slowly incorporate the flour, cheese, paprika, cumin, & hot sauce. Cover the bowl & place in the frig for 2 hours or longer.
2. Rinse the olives & then pat dry, using some paper towels.
3. Pinch off a piece of the cream mixture (about the size of one of the olives, flatten the cheese mixture on a piece of parchment paper, then place an olive in the center, & carefully wrap the olive in the cream mixture. Repeat with remaining olives.
4. Place the olives in the freezer for an hour, then remove & let stand at room temperature for approximately 15 minutes.
5. In a preheated oven set to 400° f. place the olives on a parchment-lined baking sheet, & bake for 15 minutes.
6. Remove from oven & let cool till slightly warm. Serve at room temperature to slightly warm.

## Plate/Present

Place the slightly warm olives on a large plate, and then have smaller plates handy, so your guests can grab a few bites.

## Try This

I like to take the green olives, and stuff them with cream cheese, or take a bit of Prosciutto, and stuff it in before wrapping...

## Plan/Purchase

### Ingredients

| | |
|---|---|
| 1/2 | c. butter, at room temperature |
| 1 | c. all-purpose flour, sifted |
| 2 | c. shredded sharp cheddar cheese |
| 1 | t. paprika |
| 1/2 | t. ground cumin |
| 1/4 | t. Franks hot pepper sauce (or your favorite) |
| 40 | green olives, large without pimento |

### Did You Know

*Dry spices have a tendency to lose their flavor after about 6 months. For the best kick, make sure that your spices are not as old as your great-great grandmother.*

*When you open the spice, write the date, plus six months on the label. That way you'll know when to replace it.*

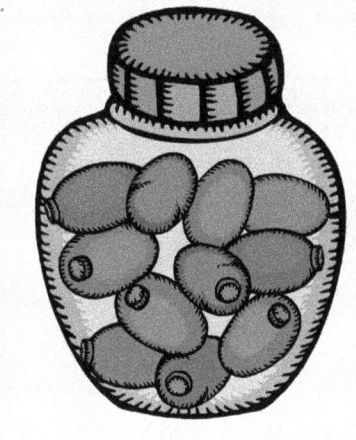

~ 63 ~

*starter*        Plan · Purchase · Prep · Prepare · Plate · Present

# Cheese & Apples with apple conserve sauce

*This is a great beginning to a meal that combines a sharp cheddar with apples for contrast, and walnuts for crunch. If you've never experienced a bite of apple with cheese, then you're in for a pleasant and tasteful surprise.*

*The sharpness of the cheese mixes with the sweetness of the apple to make your mouth go WOW, plus the walnuts help to bring the tastes together.*

## Plan/Purchase

### Cheese & Apple Bites

| | |
|---|---|
| 1 | batch Apple Conserve |
| 8 | rectangular slices sharp white cheddar, about 2-1/2 inch by 1-1/2 inch by 1/4 inch thick (about 1/2 ounce per slice) |

### Apple Conserve:

| | |
|---|---|
| 2/3 | c. peeled and diced green apple |
| 2/3 | c. peeled and diced red apple |
| 1/2 | c. brown sugar, firmly-packed |
| 1/3 | c. golden raisins |
| 1/4 | c. walnuts, coarsely chopped |
| 2 | T. balsamic vinegar |

## Prep/Prepare

### Apple Conserve

1. In a small saucepan combine all the ingredients for the apple conserve.
2. Cook over medium-low heat for 15 minutes, stirring occasionally.
3. Remove from heat and let cool.

## Plate/Present

Take a piece of the cheese and lay in in the center of a small plate, drizzle some of the apple conserve sauce over the cheese, and around the plate, for decoration.

Lay another piece of cheese on top at a skewed angle, garnish with walnuts and serve.

## Did You Know

There are about 30 species of apples in the North Temperate Zone, and that more apples are consumed than any other temperate-zone tree fruit. An apple an day, keeps the doctor away...

And about that cheese... Cheddar cheese is a hard, pale yellow to orange, sharp-tasting cheese originally made in the English village of Cheddar, in Somerset.

# Crab Rangoon

Crab Rangoons are deep-fried dumplings typically served in American Chinese restaurants. They're stuffed with a combination of cream cheese, lightly flaked crab meat, and scallions, wrapped in Chinese wonton wrappers, and then deep fried in vegetable oil. A side dish with soy sauce for dipping completes this tasty treat. Guests love to nosh on these tasteful bites, while anxiously awaiting for the main meal.

## Prep/Prepare

1. Mix the cream cheese, soy sauce, ginger, garlic, parsley, cilantro & crab meat, in a small bowl
2. Depending on the size of the wonton wrappers, place 1/2 to 1 t. of the cream cheese mixture into the center of each wonton wrapper.
3. Fold over the stuffing to make a triangle. Moisten the edges with a little water, & seal.
4. Heat oil in a large heavy skillet or deep fryer to 360° f.
5. Add 3 or 4 wontons to the hot oil, & cook until golden brown, turning once.
6. Set aside on paper towels to drain
7. Repeat until all wontons have been fried. Serve hot.

## Plate/Present

Place on a large plate, and let your guests have at it. Place additional soy sauce into small bowls (like prep bowls), so your guests can give them a dip.

They should be allowed to rest for a few minutes before serving; however, they should still be nice and warm.

## Prep Tip

If there will be a bit of time between the making and frying of the wontons, cover them with a slightly damp cloth, to keep them from drying out.

## Alternate

If you're not a big fan of frying, try placing the wontons on a parchment-lined baking sheet, and then bake in a pre-heated 350° f. oven for about 10 to 12 minutes.

Brushing a bit of vegetable oil on the wontons before baking helps to make them crispy.

## Plan/Purchase

### Ingredients

| | |
|---|---|
| 14 | oz. package wonton wrappers |
| 16 | oz. cream cheese, softened |
| 1 | t. minced fresh ginger root |
| 1/2 | t. chopped fresh cilantro |
| 1/2 | t. dried parsley |
| 3 | T. dark soy sauce |
| 1 | lb. fresh crabmeat, picked over for shell fragments, and shredded |
| 1 | qt. oil for frying |

### Did You Know

Soy sauce is one of the world's oldest condiments. It has been used in China for more than 2,500 years.

Soy sauce it traditionally made by fermenting a mixture of mashed soybeans, salt, and enzymes.

*starter*     Plan · Purchase · Prep · Prepare · Plate · Present

# Stuffed Mushrooms

Stuffed mushrooms have been decorating party plates since the fifties, and way before. This particular version of the age-old classic adds a bit of kick to a tried and true favorite, and brings this starter dish crashing into the 21st century.

You won't find any bread crumbs (a traditional ingredient) in these beauties, just a lot of great flavor that will have your guests clamoring for the recipe.

## Plan/Purchase

### Ingredients

- 12 fresh whole mushrooms, white buton
- 1 T. light olive oil
- 1 T. garlic, minced
- 1 green onion, white part chopped.
- 8 oz. cream cheese, at room temperature
- 1/4 c. Parmesan cheese, grated
- 1/4 t. freshly ground black pepper
- 1/4 t. onion powder
- 1/4 t. cayenne pepper

### Preparation Tip

These mushroom caps can be made up to two days before the party, and simply popped into the oven. Make sure to keep them tightly covered in the frig, or they'll dry out on you.

### Chef's Tip

Instead of finely chopping the mushroom stems, simply cut off the woody ends, and use a food processor fitted with a steel blade.

## Prep/Prepare

1. Place a rack in the middle position of the oven, & then preheat to 350° f.
2. Brush mushrooms to remove any dirt, or wipe with a damp paper towel.
3. Remove stems, & finely chop. If the ends are dried out, discard before chopping.
4. Preheat a pan over medium heat, coat with the oil, & then add the garlic, green onion, and chopped mushroom stems.
5. Saute until all the moisture is removed (make sure that the garlic does not burn).
6. Allow the mixture to cool in a large bowl.
7. After cooling, incorporate the cream cheese, Parmesan cheese, black pepper, onion powder & cayenne pepper.
8. Fill each mushroom cap with the mixture & allow to slightly overflow.
9. Place the mushroom caps on a parchment-lined baking sheet
10. Bake for 20 minutes.

## Additions

If you're into crab, this is an excellent addition to this recipe. Simply add about 8 ounces of chunk crab meat in step 7. However, if you're using crab, you'll want to serve them the same day.

## Assembling

The consistency of this mixture (if you're not using any crab) makes a perfect candidate for the use of a pastry bag. Just fill the bag, use a large tip, and pipe the mixture into the mushrooms. Easy, fast, and less messy.

# Cucumber Sandwiches

*These open-faced appetizers are easy to make, and a great treat to get the festivities started. I enjoy serving them in the summertime, as a starter for a day of outdoor fun. They're great on a hot summer day, and they don't fill you up. The traditional version of this sandwich is composed of paper-thin slices of cucumber placed between two triangular slices of lightly buttered white bread. This recipe takes tradition and stands it on its head.*

*When you have a party, and bring out these sandwiches, you'll be assured of happy guests.*

## Prep/Prepare

1. Blend the cream cheese, sour cream & Italian-style salad dressing mix, in a small non-reactive bowl.
2. Spread a tablespoon of the cream cheese mixture onto a slice of cocktail rye.
3. Top with a slice of cucumber.

## Plate/Present

Use a large serving plate, and arrange the open-faced sandwiches in a decorative pattern.

Place the plate on your sideboard or other serving area, and keep a supply of small cocktail napkins near for your guests to grab.

## Did You Know

Cucumber sandwiches are served during tea break at club cricket matches in England... Tally Ho.

## Chef's Tip

To get uniformly thin slices of cucumber use a mandolin. If, however, a mandolin is not in your kitchen, use a large knife, like a chef's knife. Just make sure that the knife is sharp, and keep you fingers away from the blade.

## Plan/Purchase

### Ingredients

| | |
|---|---|
| 8 | oz. package cream cheese, softened |
| 3 | T. sour cream |
| 1 | package dry Italian-style salad dressing mix |
| 1 | loaf cocktail rye bread |
| 2 | cucumbers, sliced |

### For Your Information

Cucumber sandwiches are considered a delicate food. Therefore, slice the bread as thinly as possible.

The peel of the cucumber should be removed or scored lengthwise with a fork before slicing.

In addition, the slices of cucumber should be dried gently with a paper towel before use.

### Did You Know

Cucumber sandwiches have been associated with the Victorian era upper classes of the United Kingdom, whose members were largely at leisure and, could afford to consume foods with little nutritional value... my, my.

*starter*            Plan · Purchase · Prep · Prepare · Plate · Present

# Cocktail Meatballs

Not only is this appetizer easy to make, the sauce they're simmered in makes for a tasty treat that will have your guests asking for more. However, be careful, because with all that good food coming you don't want to fill up their stomachs with appetizers.

The combination of grape jelly with the mustard and chili sauce really help to give these meatballs a proper kick.

## Plan/Purchase

### Ingredients

| | |
|---|---|
| 1 | lb. ground beef |
| 1 | egg, slightly beaten |
| 2 | T. water |
| 1/2 | c. bread crumbs |
| 3 | T. minced onion |
| 10 | oz. grape jelly |
| 1/4 | c. chili sauce |
| 2 | T. prepared mustard |

### Chef's Tip

Once the meatballs are baked you can finish this recipe out in a crock pot, and let your guests grab directly out of the pot.

Now, that's what I call an easy appetizer.

## Prep/Prepare

1. Preheat oven to 350° f.
2. Line a baking sheet with parchment paper.
3. Combine the ground beef with the egg, water, minced onion & bread crumbs.
4. Shape ground beef into golf-size balls.
5. Place on baking sheet, & bake for 20 to 25 minutes until done.
6. Drain the meatballs by placing on a paper towel.
7. Heat the jelly, chili sauce and mustard together in a 2 qt. Dutch oven.
8. Add the meatballs to the Dutch oven. Cover & simmer on low for 1/2 hour.

## Plate/Present

Serve hot in chaffing dish, and have small dishes for guests to use. Add some toothpicks for picking, some napkins for wiping, and you've got it.

Cooking with a Plan Vol 1: Back to the Kitchen  *starter*

# Baked Potato Skins

*I like potato skins; however, some variations on this classic recipe leave the skins limp and tasteless. This recipe keeps the skins firm, and the ingredients are lip-smacking good... two things that I consider very important when making potato skins.*

*As with all classics, this starter has about as many variations as there are chefs. This recipe is one that I came up with, and my guests seem to like them. However, feel free to add your own special touches.*

## Prep/Prepare

1. Scrub & clean the potatoes
2. Rub the skins with oil & salt.
3. Position the rack to the middle position, & then preheat to 425° f.
4. Bake for 90 minutes (an inserted fork should enter cleanly & smoothly.
5. Cut potatoes in half lengthwise; & scoop out the flesh, leaving the shell about 1/4 inch thick.
6. Place cut side down on a parchment-lined baking sheet.
7. Mix oil, Parmesan cheese, salt, garlic powder, paprika & pepper in a small bowl, and then brush over both sides of skins.
8. Bake at 475 f. for 6 minutes, then turn & bake another 6 minutes, or until crisp.
9. Sprinkle bacon and cheddar cheese inside skins, & bake for 3 minutes (cheese should be fully melted).

## Plate/Present

Place on a large serving plate, top with sour cream and onions, and then stand back.

## Plan/Purchase

### Ingredients

| | |
|---|---|
| 4 | large baking potatoes |
| 3 | T. vegetable oil |
| 1 | T. grated Parmesan cheese |
| 1/2 | t. salt |
| 1/4 | t. garlic powder |
| 1/4 | t. paprika |
| 1/8 | t. pepper |
| 8 | bacon strips, cooked and crumbled |
| 1 1/2 | c. shredded sharp Cheddar cheese |
| 1/2 | c. sour cream |
| 4 | green onions, sliced (just the green parts) |

### Chef's Tip

*There are all kinds of potatoes... this recipe works best with russet potatoes.*

~ 69 ~

Plan · Purchase · Prep · Prepare · Plate · Present / Starter

# Awesome Guacamole

This is one of my favorite appetizers. It's easy to make, and the guests gobble it up. However, there have been parties that I've attended where the guacamole was abysmal. The secret to good guacamole is in getting the right (fresh) ingredients (it's always about the ingredients).

The final product will not be anything like that store-bought goop, but a fresh combination of smooth and chunky avocado, with just the right combination of spices.

## Plan/Purchase

### Ingredients

| | | |
|---|---|---|
| 3 | | medium Hass avocados, ripe |
| 2 | T. | minced onion |
| 1 | T. | minced garlic |
| 1 | t. | minced jalapeño chile |
| 1/4 | c. | minced fresh cilantro |
| 1/4 | t. | table salt |
| 1/2 | t. | ground cumin |
| 2 | T. | lime juice |

### Chef's Tip

Avocados can turn brown quickly. So you should prep all the other ingredients first.

### For Your Information

How can you tell when an avocado is ripe? Pick it up and press your thumb into the skin. If it feels like the Rock of Gilbratar put it down. If it gives slightly, and leaves an indentation, that avocado is ready.

~ 70 ~

## Prep/Prepare

1. Cut two of the avocados in half, remove pits, & use a spoon to scoop the flesh into a bowl.
2. Using the tines of a fork, mash the flesh with all the ingredients, except the lime juice
3. Cut the last avocado in half, remove the pit, and then use a small knife to cut the flesh into cubes.
4. Gently remove the cubes with a spoon, add them to the bowl, add the lime juice, & gently combine. The mixture should now be smooth with chunky bits.
5. Adjust seasoning with salt and/or lime juice, if necessary.

## Plate/Present

Put the guacamole into a colorful bowl, place it in the middle of a large plate, and then surround it with your favorite chips. Cut a lime, into wedges, and then place into a small bowl. Serve immediately.

## Additions

It is possible to store guacamole for up to one day in the refrigerator. Just make sure that you press a piece of plastic wrap onto the surface of the mixture. The mixture should be returned to room temperature before serving.

## Dip versus Dollop

There's two schools of thought on serving guacamole. Do you allow your guests to dip into a community bowl, or do you give them small plates, and let them spoon out a dollop of their own?

In my case I prefer the latter, because that gives me a chance to add a bit more lime to my guacamole (I like extra lime). However, it really doesn't matter when you're with friends. Just remember... no double dipping, please.

Cooking with a Plan Vol 1: Back to the Kitchen  *starter*

# Not So Classic Spinach Dip

*Spinach dip was a classic at parties in the fifties. Over the years it died out, and became the butt of many jokes. As a matter of fact, there were so many variations of the dish, you could write a cookbook called variations on spinach dip.*

*This recipe is no joke, and the flavor it packs will bring life back to an old fifties standard. Just give it a try, and I think you'll see what I mean.*

## Prep/Prepare

1. Partially thaw the spinach (outside should be soft with the interior icy, but breakable).
2. Squeeze the spinach of excess water.
3. Use a food processor, to process spinach, with other ingredients (except salt) until smooth.
4. Transfer to serving bowl & add salt, to taste. (Dip can be covered with plastic wrap and refrigerated up to 2 days.)

## Plate/Present

Put the dip into a serving bowl, and surround it with your favorite goodies.

As a matter of fact, my favorite way to serve this dip is in a slightly toasted bread bowl. Not only is the bread bowl, great for presentation, but when all the dip has been extracted, the guests can eat the bowl… no cleanup.

## Chef's Tip

This dip fares well in the refrigerator, and will last for up to two days, if tightly covered.

## Did You Know

You can use the microwave, to partially thaw the spinach. Just remember to use the low setting, and keep an eye on it so it doesn't cook. When the outside is soft, and the inside is still a bit icy, you're there.

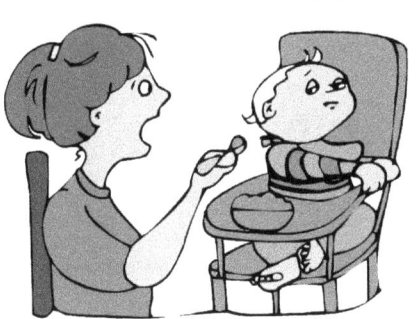

## Plan/Purchase

### Ingredients

| | | |
|---|---|---|
| 10 | oz. | frozen chopped spinach |
| 1/2 | c. | sour cream |
| 1/2 | c. | mayonnaise |
| 2 | T. | thin-sliced scallions, white parts only |
| 1 | T. | chopped fresh dill |
| 1/2 | c. | packed flat-leaf parsley |
| 1 | t. | garlic, minced |
| 1/4 | t. | ground black pepper |
| 2 | T. | fresh oregano leaves |
| 2 | oz. | feta cheese, crumbled |
| 1 | T. | lemon juice |
| 1 | t. | grated lemon zest |
| | | salt, to taste |

### For Your Information

*Instead of using a serving bowl, you could get a large round-shaped loaf of bread, tear out the insides, and use that as a bowl.*

~ 71 ~

# Beef & Pork

That beef comes from cows is known to most, but the close relationship between the words beef and cow is hardly household knowledge. Cow comes via Middle English from Old English cü, which is descended from the Indo-European root *gwou–, also meaning "cow." This root has descendants in most of the branches of the Indo-European language family. Among those descendants is the Latin word bös, "cow," whose stem form, bov-, eventually became the Old French word buef, also meaning "cow." The French nobles who ruled England after the Norman Conquest of course used French words to refer to the meats they were served, so the animal called cü by the Anglo-Saxon peasants was called buef by the French nobles when it was brought to them cooked at dinner. Thus arose the distinction between the words for animals and their meat that is also found in the English word-pairs swine/pork, sheep/mutton, and deer/venison. What is interesting about cow/beef is that we are in fact dealing with one and the same word, etymologically speaking.

Now, after reading that, don't you feel better?

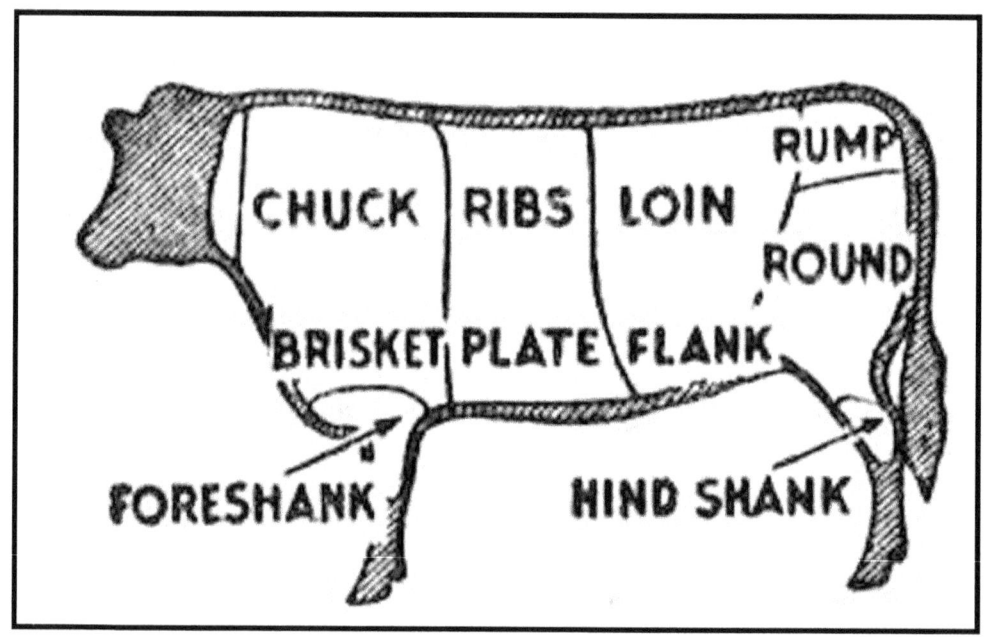

# It's What's for Dinner

The tried-but-true saying that everything but the pig's squeal can be used is accurate indeed. Though pigs are bred primarily for their meat (commonly referred to as pork) and fat, the trimmings and lesser cuts (feet, jowl, tail, etc.) are used for sausage, the bristles for brushes, the hair for furniture and the skin for leather. The majority of pork in the marketplace today is cured-like bacon and ham-while the remainder is termed "fresh." Slaughterhouses can (but usually don't) request and pay for their pork to be graded by the U.S. Department of Agriculture (USDA). The grades are USDA 1, 2, 3, 4 and utility-from the best downwards-based on the proportion of lean to fat. Whether graded or not, all pork used for intrastate commerce is subjected to state or federal inspection for wholesomeness, insuring that the slaughter and processing of the animal was done under sanitary conditions. Pork shipped interstate must be federally inspected. Today's pork is leaner (about 1/3 fewer calories) and higher in protein than that consumed just 10 years ago. Thanks to improved feeding techniques, trichinosis in pork is now also rarely an issue. Normal precautions should still be taken, however, such as washing anything (hands, knives, cutting boards, etc.) that comes in contact with raw pork and never tasting uncooked pork. Cooking it to an internal temperature of 137°F will kill any trichinae. However, allowing for a safety margin for thermometer inaccuracy, most experts recommend an internal temperature of from 150° to 165°F, which will still produce a juicy, tender result.

Because of the leaner nature of today's pork, it is recommended that many cuts of pork be brined before cooking.

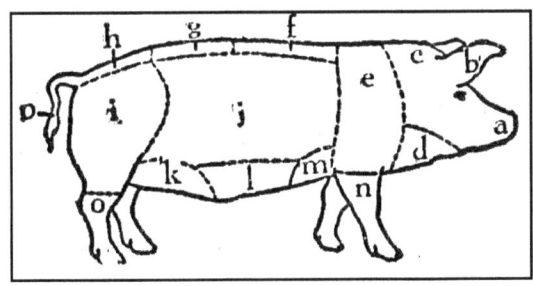

main dish                    Plan · Purchase · Prep · Prepare · Plate · Present

# Tasty Corned Beef with apricot sauce

*This is an awesome recipe, with a mouth-watering apricot sauce that really brings out the flavor in corned beef. Old-fashioned corned beef is grayish-pink in color and very salty; the newer style has less salt and is a bright rosy red.*

*Although I'm a follower of tradition, I prefer the newer style of beef; it tastes great, and many versions of it are now made without the use of nitrates... and that's a good thing.*

## Plan/Purchase

### Ingredients

- 4 1/2 lb. corned beef, rinsed
- 1 c. water
- 1 c. apricot preserves
- 4 T. brown sugar
- 2 T. soy sauce

### Did You Know

The Oxford English Dictionary dates the usage of "corn," 888 AD, and the term "corned beef" to 1621.

In Britain, corned beef is usually bought at the delicatessen, or may be found in trapezoid cans, imported from South America

## Prep/Prepare

1. Preheat oven to 350° f.
2. Place the corned beef in a baking dish and add water.
3. Cover, bake for 2 hours, & then drain liquid.
4. In a small bowl combine apricot preserves, brown sugar, & soy sauce. Spread the apricot mixture evenly over the corned beef.
5. Bake uncovered at 350° f. for 25 to 30 more minutes; baste occasionally with pan drippings.

## Plate/Present

Slice corned beef across the grain and serve with cabbage and some red potatoes.

## Did You Know

Corned beef was originally a substitute for Irish bacon in the late 1800s. Irish immigrants living in New York City's Lower East Side sought an equivalent in taste and texture to their traditional Irish bacon, and learned about this cheaper alternative to bacon from their Jewish neighbors. Don't you just love trivia...

Cooking with a Plan Vol 1: Back to the Kitchen  *main dish*

# Ultimate Stuffed Pork Chops

*If you like the other white meat and you also happen to like stuffing (but you only get some at Thanksgiving), then you're going to love this recipe. It's great comfort food, and fit for everything from dining alone, to serving up to a hungry crowd.*

*Pork chops are actually steak-style cuts of pork from the loin of the pig. Modern day pork has a tendency to be a bit dry; hence the brining of the pork before cooking... do not skip this important step.*

## *Prep/Prepare*

1. Using a sharp knife, cut a pocket into each pork chop.
2. Brine the chops (See Appendix B: Techniques).
3. To make the stuffing, melt butter in a skillet over medium heat until foaming subsides.
4. Add onions, celery, & salt and cook until veggies are tender (about 10m).
5. Add garlic & herbs and cook until fragrant (about 1m). Transfer to medium bowl, add bread cubes, cream & pepper, and toss until combined... set aside.
6. To make the chops. Preheat oven to 450f, and adjust rack to lower-middle position.
7. Remove chops from brine, pat dry, & add about 1/3 cup of dressing to the pocket of each chop.
8. Season the chops with pepper, & brown in a skillet over high heat until a nice crust has formed (about 3 minutes), turn the chops & repeat for the other side (another 2 or 3 minutes).
9. Transfer the chops to a rimmed baking sheet, lined with parchment paper, & roast until an instant-read thermometer inserted into the center of the stuffing reads 130f (about 15m). Turn the chops once during the baking period.
10. Transfer the chops to a plate, loosely tent with foil, & let rest for about 5m. An instant-read thermometer should read an internal temperature of 145f.

## *Plate/Present*

The plating does not have to be fancy... this is good old-fashioned comfort food. In fact, you might want to serve this dish family style. Place all the chops on one plate (using a plate warmer, or sticking the serving plate in the oven for a minute or two, will help to keep the chops at temperature). Then place stewed apples or some garlic mashed in another big bowl. Toss some lettuce with some oil, vinegar, and Parmesan cheese in another bowl. Then stand back and let your guests serve themselves.

## *Plan/Purchase*

### The Pork Chops & Brine

| | |
|---|---|
| 4 | bone-in rib loin pork chops 1 1/2 inches thick (about 12 oz. each) |
| 3/4 | c. packed light brown sugar |
| 1/2 | c. kosher salt (Diamond Crystal), or 1/4 c. table salt |
| - | ground black pepper, to taste |
| 2 | T. vegetable oil |

### The Stuffing

| | |
|---|---|
| 3 | T. unsalted butter |
| 1 | small onion, diced small |
| 1 | medium rib of celery, diced small |
| 1/2 | t. table salt |
| 2 | cloves garlic, minced |
| 2 | t. minced fresh thyme leaves |
| 1 | T. minced fresh parsley leaves |
| 2 | c. bread cubes (1/4 inch cubes) from 1 baguette |
| 2 | T. heavy cream |
| 1/8 | t. ground black pepper |

### Preparation Tip

*To make the pocket cut, lay the chop down, place one hand on top, and then use a sharp knife to cut into the chop.*

*Cut to the left and right, and cut deep, but be careful not to cut all the way through the chop.*

*main dish*  Plan · Purchase · Prep · Prepare · Plate · Present

# Korean Barbecued Beef

Korean beef, or Pulgogi as it's know in Korea, is traditionally prepared on a small grill right at the table. The meat is tender, and the mixture of the soy sauces and sugar compliment the chili sauce.

Sriracha (SEE-rah-chah) is the generic name for a Southeast Asian hot sauce from Thailand. If you're having trouble locating this sauce, one of the most famous brands is made by Huy Fong Foods, an American company, that puts an emblem of a rooster on the bottle. You can find them on the Web at http://www.huyfong.com.

## Plan/Purchase

### Ingredients

| | |
|---|---|
| 1 1/2 | lb. beef tenderloin, about 5 inches thick |
| 4 | garlic cloves, chopped |
| 1.5 | T. sugar, granulated |
| 6 | T. light soy sauce |
| 1 | T. dark soy sauce |
| 1.5 | T. Asian sesame oil |
| 2 | T. rice vinegar |
| 5 | green onions, minced, plus shredded green onion for garnish |
| 1 | t. grated peeled fresh ginger |
| 2 | T. sesame seeds, toasted and crushed |
| 1/2 | t. freshly ground black pepper |
| 2 | T. water |
| 1 | t. Sriracha chili sauce |
| 1 | T. canola oil |

## Prep/Prepare

1. Cut the beef across the grain into slices 1/8 inch thick.
2. Mash together three-fourths of the chopped garlic & 1 Tbs. sugar, forming a paste.
3. Place the paste in a bowl & stir in 3 T. light & dark soy sauce, 1 T. sesame oil, 1 T. vinegar, all but 1 T. of the minced green onions, the ginger, 1 T. sesame seeds, all the black pepper & 1 T. water.
4. Place the beef in shallow bowl & pour marinade on top.
5. Mix well, cover & refrigerate about 3 hours.
6. Combine the rest of the chopped garlic & 1/2 T. sugar, to form a paste.
7. Place paste in a bowl and whisk in the remaining light soy sauce, vinegar, chili sauce, 1 t. sesame oil, minced green onions, sesame seeds & the remaining 1 T. water.
8. Set aside until ready to serve.
9. Remove the beef from the marinade & pat dry.
10. Arrange the beef in a single layer on a grill over high heat.
11. Sear, turning once, until crisp & brown on both sides, about 2 minutes per side. Wipe & oil the rack between batches, if necessary.

## Plate/Present

Transfer to a warmed platter, garnish with the shredded green onion and serve immediately with the dipping sauce... This dish has fantastic taste.

*Cooking with a Plan Vol I: Back to the Kitchen*  *main dish*

# Melt-in-Your-Mouth Pork Roast

*This is a great recipe for preparing a fantastic pork roast. Follow the recipe, as outlined, and keep an eye on the internal temperature of the roast... If you go over 150° f, the roast will be too dry.*

*Although you can use a bone-in roast, this recipe works best with a nice boneless pork roast. To make this roast even more juicy, you might try brining the roast ahead of time. Check Appendix A: Brining, for more information on this technique.*

## Prep/Prepare

1. Place the roast in a baking dish, rub with olive oil, & then rub the spices into the meat.
2. Cover, & let the roast rest in the refrigerator for 1 to 2 hours.
3. Place rack in the middle position, & then preheat oven to 350° f.
4. Cook pork roast about 1 hour, or to an internal temperature of 140 f. is reached.
5. Remove from oven and allow to rest for 15 minutes before carving.

## Plate/Present

Some white rice, black beans, a few pan fried plantains or some roast potatoes and apple sauce.

## What is Resting?

Once a roast, or other meat dish, is removed from the oven, the juices are concentrated inside the meat. When the meat rests, the juices will begin to redistribute equally throughout the dish; making for a flavorful, and juicy meal.

## Plan/Purchase

### Ingredients

| | |
|---|---|
| 1 1/2 | **T. fresh rosemary** |
| 2 | **t. garlic salt** |
| 1/2 | **t. dried thyme** |
| 1/4 | **t. freshly ground black pepper** |
| 3 | **lb. boneless pork loin roast** |

### Chef's Tip

*Pork roast will dry out very fast, if it's over cooked. Therefore an internal meat thermometer is a must. Stop the cooking when the internal temperature of the roast reaches 140° f.*

*As the roast rests, the internal temperature will raise another 6 to 8 degrees... internal cooking will finish the job.*

*main dish*        Plan · Purchase · Prep · Prepare · Plate · Present

# Stick-to-your-ribs Irish Stew

*A St. Patrick's Day dinner, for sure; however, you don't have to wait for the wearing of the green to enjoy this tasty dish, you can have it any time you please.*

*A traditional Irish stew is a layered dish of equal parts seasoned lamb or mutton chops, potatoes and onions. I took some liberties with this recipe, by using some good beef stew meat. In addition, I added some carrots to help compliment the flavor of the beef.*

## Plan/Purchase

### Ingredients

| | |
|---|---|
| 2 | lb. lean beef stew meat, cubed |
| 3 | T. vegetable oil, divided |
| 2 | T. all-purpose flour |
| - | freshly ground black pepper to taste |
| 1 | pinch cayenne pepper |
| 2 | large onions, chopped |
| 1 | clove garlic, crushed |
| 2 | T. tomato paste |
| 1 1/2 | c. Irish stout beer (e.g., Guinness) |
| 2 | c. chopped carrot |
| 2 | c. cubed red potatoes |
| 1 | sprig fresh thyme |
| 1 | T. chopped fresh parsley for garnish |

### Chef's Tip

*Those bits at the bottom of the pan, you're scraping at (step 8) are called fonds, and as they dissolve, they will add tremendous flavor to the dish.*

## Prep/Prepare

1. Combine the flour, salt, pepper, & cayenne pepper in a bowl.
2. Toss the beef cubes with 1 tablespoon of vegetable oil, & then dredge the beef in in the flour mixture.
3. Heat the remaining oil in a large skillet or Dutch oven using medium-high heat.
4. Add the beef, & brown on all sides.
5. Add onions, & garlic to the beef.
6. Dilute the tomato paste with a small amount of water, pour into the pan & stir to blend.
7. Reduce the heat to medium, cover, and cook for 5 minutes.
8. Pour 1/2 cup of the beer into the pan, & as it begins to boil, scrape any bits of food from the bottom of the pan with a wooden spoon.
9. Pour in the rest of the beer, & add the carrots, potatoes and thyme.
10. Cover, reduce heat to low, & simmer for 2 to 3 hours, stirring occasionally.

## Plate/Present

Taste and adjust seasoning before serving. Garnish with chopped parsley, and use big bowls. Add a loaf of country bread with butter, and you're all set to go.

~ 78 ~

Cooking with a Plan Vol I: Back to the Kitchen  main dish

# Tender Beef Tips with kidney beans

*This is an excellent dish, and the long simmering time makes for fork tender beef. The skillet or dutch oven that you use should be big enough to hold all of the ingredients, and give the beef enough room to brown without simply steaming.*

*Flap meat steak (a.k.a top sirloin tips, or beef sirloin tips,) give great beefy flavor and are reasonably tender. Although I'm not a fan of powdered anything, if you want to save a bit of time, you could try some of the package gravy mixes. Or you could do what I do... mix up a roux, and make your own.*

## Prep/Prepare

1. Heat a large skillet, or dutch oven, over high heat.
2. Add onions & saute until translucent (10 minutes).
3. Add the stew meat & cook on high heat until meat is browned on all sides (5 minutes).
4. Add water, soy, & Worcestershire sauce.
5. Stir in garlic powder, salt & pepper.
6. Bring to a boil & then reduce heat.
7. Simmer (covered) for 1 1/2 to 2 hours.
8. Make the gravy (choice is up to you).
9. Mix thoroughly & stir into the meat mixture.
10. Return to a boil stirring frequently until slightly thickened.

## Plate/Present

This is an excellent dish, served over rice or egg noodles, and if dry gravy mixes are not you're style, you can always make your own from scratch.

## Plan/Purchase

### Beef Tips

| | |
|---|---|
| 3 | T. vegetable oil |
| 1 | onion, chopped |
| 2 | lb. cubed beef stew meat |
| 2 | c. water |
| 1/4 | c. soy sauce |
| 1/4 | c. Worcestershire sauce |
| 1 | t. garlic powder |
| 1 | t, salt |
| 1 | t. ground black pepper |

### Gravy

| | |
|---|---|
| 1 | package of brown gravy mix |
| 1 | c. water |

~ 79 ~

main dish  Plan · Purchase · Prep · Prepare · Plate · Present

# Beef and Pepper Saute

This is a great dish to put together for a special evening meal, and you won't make much of a mess in the process. The peppers add a bit of a bite to the dish, and also a bit of color.

Speaking of color... The color of a bell pepper is not aesthetic, it denotes the age of the pepper. Green peppers are unripe, while the other colors, red, yellow, and orange are harvested later. As a bell pepper ages, its flavor becomes sweeter and milder. Green peppers have twice the amount of vitamin C by weight than citrus fruits... but I still like my glass of orange juice in the morning.

## Plan/Purchase

### Ingredients

| | |
|---|---|
| 1 | c. dry jasmine rice |
| 2 | c. water |
| 1 | lb. lean ground beef |
| 1 | T. olive oil |
| 1 | red bell pepper, sliced |
| 1 | green bell pepper, sliced |
| 1/4 | c. chopped fresh parsley |
| 2 | large cloves garlic, thinly sliced |
| 2 | T. minced fresh ginger root |
| 1/4 | t. crushed red pepper |
| 1/4 | t. salt |
| 1/4 | t. ground black pepper |
| 1/4 | c. beef stock |
| 1 | T. low-sodium soy sauce |
| 1 | t. chile paste |
| 1/2 | t. Worcestershire sauce |

### For Your Information

Bell peppers contain a recessive gene that eliminates the capsaicin in the fruit meaning that they have none of the "heat" that many other varieties of peppers possess.

## Prep/Prepare

1. Cut open and remove the seeds from the peppers, and then cut into 1/4 thick slices.
2. Bring the rice and water to a boil, in a medium saucepan. Cover, reduce heat, & simmer 20 minutes, or according to package directions.
3. Cook & stir the ground beef until evenly browned in a large skillet over medium heat. Drain, & set aside.
4. Heat the olive oil in the same skillet over medium heat.
5. Stir in the red bell &, green bell pepper, parsley, garlic & ginger. Season with red pepper, salt, & pepper. Cook & stir until tender.
6. Return the beef to the skillet. Mix in the beef stock, soy sauce, chile paste, and Worcestershire sauce.
7. Cook & stir until thickened & heated through.

## Plate/Present

Place a mound of rice in the center of the plate and then scoop a generous amount of the beef/pepper dish, right on top.

You might even drizzle a bit of the sauce around the plate, for decoration.

Cooking with a Plan Vol 1: Back to the Kitchen — main dish

# Shepherd's Pie with beef & noodles

*Shepherd's pie is an Irish dish that traditionally consists of a bottom layer of minced (ground) meat in gravy covered with mashed potato and (optionally) a layer of cheese. It's a great dish to feed a batch of hungry folk.*

*The meat is traditionally lamb (hence Shepherd) although in North America it is often made with minced (ground) beef which is also known as a cottage pie.*

*To make this dish even more interesting, I've add some elbow macaroni.*

## Prep/Prepare

1. Place oven rack in the middle position, & then preheat to 425° f.
2. Brown the beef in a skillet, using medium high heat & drain thoroughly.
3. Add the water, soup mix and elbow macaroni, & then simmer for 5 minutes.
4. Pour mixture into a 9x13 inch baking dish.
5. Top with potatoes & sprinkle with paprika.
6. Bake for 15 to 20 minutes & serve hot.

## Plate/Present

Some dishes are just best served casual. So, don't plate this dish, just present it. Stick it in the middle of the table with a nice big spoon, give your guests some plates, and let them get their own.

## Plan/Purchase

### Ingredients

| | |
|---|---|
| 1 | lb. ground beef |
| 1.5 | c. hot water |
| 1 | package beef/onion soup mix |
| 1/2 | c. uncooked elbow macaroni |
| 2 | c. homemade mashed potatoes |
| 1/2 | t. paprika |

### Chef's Tip

*To prevent the mashed potatoes from sinking into the layer of meat, lighten them by whipping milk, butter and/or air into them before adding.*

main dish — Plan · Purchase · Prep · Prepare · Plate · Present

# Pork Ribs Texas Style

*Pork ribs make for a great main dish... hot off the smoking grill, they are the kind of food that requires a good appetite and plenty of paper towels and wet naps.*

*Although this recipe requires the ribs to marinate overnight, the work involved is pretty much straight forward and easy to accomplish. The smoking of the ribs is best done on a charcoal grill; however, if you work with gas, don't worry, I have a way for you to generate good smoky ribs.*

*Okay, bibs at the ready, let's get cooking... Texas style, that is.*

## Plan/Purchase

### Ingredients

| | |
|---|---|
| 6 | lb. pork spareribs |
| 1.5 | c. granulated sugar |
| 1/4 | c. salt |
| 2 1/2 | T. ground black pepper |
| 3 | T. paprika |
| 1 | t. cayenne pepper |
| 2 | T. garlic powder |
| 6 | T. pan drippings |
| 1/2 | c. chopped onion |
| 4 | c. ketchup |
| 3 | c. hot water |
| 4 | T. brown sugar |
| | salt and pepper to taste |
| 1 | c. wood chips, soaked |

### Chef's Tip

*Most BBQ pros add some of the sauce just at the last minute or two of grilling, or they (as I suggest) don't grill with the sauce at all, and offer it as a side when eating the meal.*

## Prep/Prepare

1. Clean & trim the ribs of excess fat.
2. Combine the sugar, 1/4 cup salt, ground black pepper, paprika, 1 tsp. cayenne pepper, & garlic powder in a small bowl, & cover the ribs with the mix.
3. Place the ribs in a oven safe pan, wrap tightly, & place in the refrigerator overnight.
4. Place the rack into the lower position of your oven, & then preheat to 270° f.
5. Uncover the ribs, place into the oven & then bake for 4 hours, or until tender.
6. Take 6 tablespoons of pan drippings & place them into a medium to medium high heat skillet,
7. Add the onion, & cook until translucent.
8. Add the ketchup & stir.
9. Add the water, brown sugar, pepper, and cayenne, & then season with salt, to taste.
10. Simmer for 45 minutes, adding water, if needed, to keep the sauce from overly thickening.
11. Set grill medium to medium low, &, clean and oil the grate. See appendix B: Grilling Non Stick.
12. Add the soaked wood chips over the coals. If you're using a gas grill, see appendix B: Turning your gas grill into a smoker.
13. Place the ribs on the rack, but do not overcrowd.
14. Grill for 20 to 30 minutes, & turn occasionally. Make sure to leave the grill cover closed, to keep the smoke inside the grill.

## Plate/Present

Place the ribs on a big platter (that's Texas style), and put the sauce into a bowl. Avoid using the sauce to baste the ribs while on the grill. In most cases this will only caramelize the sugars and cause the sauce to burn.

Cooking with a Plan Vol I: Back to the Kitchen — main dish

# Slow Cooked Beef Stew

*This is an extremely simple recipe to prepare; however, it's not something that you will prepare at the spur of the moment. Once the tasty ingredients are placed in the pot, all you have to do is stick it in the oven and wait... about six hours.*

*I promise you, that the wait will be well worth it when you see the happy looks on the faces of your guests, as they dig into this stew, and then ask for another bowl... can I have some more, please.*

*Just make sure you get some for yourself, because with this recipe, there won't be much left over.*

## Prep/Prepare

1. Toss the beef with flour, salt & pepper,
2. Add beef to an oven-proof pot or Dutch oven, & let rest for about 5 minutes.
3. Place the rack in the lower position of your oven, & then preheat to 250° f.
4. Combine the garlic, bay leaf, paprika, Worcestershire, onion, beef broth, potatoes, carrots, & celery in a small bowl, & then pour over beef.
5. Gently stir to combine.
6. Place the covered pot into the oven, & cook for 4 to 6 hours, until the meat is fork tender.

## Plate/Present

If you used a Dutch oven, the initial presentation can be by placing it on the table, covered, and let your guests have at it. Since the pot came out of the oven, you should place a tea towel, or pot holder over the lid, so your guests won't burn their hands.

This is basically a one-pot main dish; so all your needs, besides plates, bowls, and silverware, is a loaf or two of good crusty bread, and a slab of butter. A French loaf would be excellent, as would a ciabatta. Whatever you choose, the bread is a grand accompaniment to any stew, and is an excellent way to sop up all of that awesome gravy.

## Plan/Purchase

### Ingredients

| | |
|---|---|
| 2 | lb. beef stew meat, cut into 1 inch cubes |
| 1/4 | c. all-purpose flour |
| 1/2 | t. salt |
| 1/2 | t. ground black pepper |
| 1 | clove garlic, minced |
| 1 | bay leaf |
| 1 | t. paprika |
| 1 | t. Worcestershire sauce |
| 1 | onion, chopped |
| 1 1/2 | c. beef broth |
| 3 | medium potatoes, diced |
| 4 | medium carrots, sliced |
| 1 | stalk celery, chopped |

### For Your Information

*The word stew is said to come from the old French word "estuier" (stü), meaning to enclose.*

*Now, aren't you glad that I shared that little piece of information with you.*

# Poultry

Poultry are domesticated birds raised for food: chickens (including Cornish game hens and poussins), turkeys, ducks, and geese, plus minor species such as squab (young pigeons) and ostrich. Game birds such as quail and Canada geese can also be prepared in much the same way, although their meat is tougher than that of birds raised on farms. Chickens and ducks are among the most widely distributed food animals in the world and are part of nearly every major cuisine.

Poultry were the last major group of food animals to be domesticated. Humans likely began by raiding the nests of wild birds to steal their eggs, just as nonhuman predators do. Eventually the birds themselves were caught and kept in confinement, or, when thoroughly domesticated, allowed to range around the farmstead or village to find their own food.

Chicken, in particular, has had an increase in popularity in the United States in recent years; according to the U.S. Department of Agriculture, sales climbed from 39 pounds per capita in 1970 to 77 pounds per capita in 2000. The surge in chicken's popularity is attributable partly to its low fat content as compared to beef. Three-and-one-half ounces (one hundred grams) of roasted chicken breast with its skin removed has only 120 calories and 1.5 grams of fat, while the same serving of cooked sirloin steak has 170 calories and 6 grams of fat.

Also propelling chicken toward the center of the nation's plate is its versatility and convenience. Chicken is convenient to prepare and less likely to be ruined by overcooking than the competition. Chicken has become a kitchen favorite for cooks who are both pressed for time and somewhat inexpert at cooking.

Cost is also a major factor in the rise of poultry's popularity. In constant dollars, the wholesale price of a whole chicken dropped 50 percent from 1978 to 2000, while the price of skinless, boneless breast dropped 70 percent.

In contrast to chicken and turkey, duck, goose, squab, and other minor species are expensive and are served mainly on special occasions in the home or in high-end restaurants or restaurants specializing in ethnic cuisine. Peking duck is a mainstay of Chinese cookery, for example.

# Eat More Chicken

The most prevalent of the domestic fowl worldwide, the chicken is descended from the Red Jungle Fowl, a bird whose native territory stretches from east India to Malaysia. It is not clear exactly where the bird was first domesticated, but it has been raised by humans throughout its range since ancient times. Polynesian explorers took the chicken across the Pacific as far as Hawaii. Chickens were exported from India to China as early as the fourteenth century B.C.E. and spread to the Near East via the trade routes, and thence to Egypt, Greece, and Rome. Domestic fowl are not mentioned in the Old Testament, but the ancient Egyptians kept fowl and developed large ovens capable of incubating thousands of eggs, indicating that they had large flocks. The Greeks had chickens by the fourth century B.C.E., and many a family in ancient Athens kept a hen to produce eggs. The Romans took up the bird and carried it throughout their empire and beyond; the Germanic and Celtic tribes north of the Roman frontier had chickens before the Christian era. Both Greeks and Romans gave chickens a prominent place in their cuisine and recorded elaborate recipes for cooking them. Poultry shops were so well-established in England by the fourteenth century that their proprietors prevailed upon the authorities to prohibit country people from bringing poultry into the city to sell in the streets in competition with them. Medieval and Renaissance banquets featured chickens along with other fowl: Pope Pius V (d. 1572) gave a banquet that included chicken pie—two chickens to each pie—and spit-roasted quails and pigeons.

*main dish*   Plan · Purchase · Prep · Prepare · Plate · Present

# French Style Chicken in a Pot

*Poulet en Cocotte or chicken in a pot, is a classic, simple preparation that involves baking a whole chicken in a covered Dutch oven. Little to no liquid is added to the pot as the chicken slowly bakes in its own juices (which are served as a jus in the finished dish).*

*The times given in the recipe are designed for a 4 1/2- to 5-pound bird. However, the recipe works with a variety of sizes. A 3 1/2- to 4 1/2-pound chicken will take about 60 minutes to cook, while a 5- to 6-pound bird will take about 2 hours.*

## Plan/Purchase

### Ingredients

| | |
|---|---|
| 1 | whole chicken (4 1/2 to 5 pounds), giblets removed |
| 2 | t. kosher salt or 1 t. table salt |
| 1/4 | t. ground black pepper |
| 1 | T. olive oil |
| 1/2 | c. chopped onion |
| 1/4 | c. chopped celery |
| 6 | medium garlic cloves, peeled and trimmed |
| 1 | bay leaf |

### Chef's Tip

*If your Dutch oven is 5-quart, do not use a chicken larger than 5 pounds... it won't fit into the pot.*
*I HATE it when that happens.*

## Prep/Prepare

1. Pat chicken dry with paper towels & then season with salt & pepper.
2. Heat the olive oil in a large Dutch oven using medium heat until the oil just begins to smoke,
3. Add chicken, breast-side up, and then scatter the onion, celery, garlic, & bay leaf around the pot.
4. Cook about 8 minutes or until the bottom of the chicken & vegetables are well browned.
5. Place rack in the lower position, & then preheat the oven to 350° f.
6. Remove pot from heat; place large sheet of foil over pot & cover tightly with lid. If you have a good dutch oven, the foil will not be necessary.
7. Transfer to oven and bake for 1.5 hours, or until an instant-read thermometer registers 160° degrees inserted in thickest part of breast & 175° degrees in thickest part of thigh.
8. Transfer chicken to carving board, tent with foil, & allow to rest for 20 minutes. This helps to redistribute the juices.
9. Strain the pot juices through a fine-mesh strainer into fat separator, & then discard solids (ideally, you should have about 3/4 cup juices).
10. Allow liquid to settle, & then pour the now separated juices into a small saucepan; set over low heat, & allow to simmer for 10 minutes.

## Plate/Present

Carve the chicken.

Note: As you're caving, you will accumulate more juices... add them to the saucepan.

Place the carved chicken on a plate, and serve with the a jus on the side in a separate bowl... enjoy.

You could also place the cut chicken on a bed of garlic mashed potatoes, and a side of steamed green beans.

*Cooking with a Plan Vol I: Back to the Kitchen*  *main dish*

# Chicken Papadoris

*This is great-tasting chicken with flavors from India. A savory coconut-garlic gravy drenches the chicken breasts for an out of this world flavor.*

*And, check this out… Any leftovers can be diced, and spooned into small puff pastries for a fantastic appetizer.*

*Just think of this recipe as a dish that just keeps on giving, and giving.*

## Prep/Prepare

1. Toast pine nuts, in a skillet over medium heat. Remove from heat, & set aside.
2. Place a large skillet over medium heat to melt the butter.
3. After the foaming subsides, add chicken, and cook for 5 to 10 minutes. The juices should run clear.
4. Add onion and garlic to the skillet, & cook until tender 10 minutes). Don't let the garlic burn.
5. Add pine nuts, soy, & coconut milk.
6. Season, to taste with paprika, cumin, & curry.
7. Whisk the cornstarch & water in a small bowl, add to the skillet, & then stir until sauce thickens.

## Plate/Present

This dish is best served on a bed of basmati rice. Place a dome of rice in the center of a dish, place some of the chicken around the rice, and then spoon over some of the sauce. Serve immediately.

## Did You Know

Curry powder is widely used in Indian cooking. Authentic Indian curry powder is freshly ground each day and can vary dramatically depending on the region and the cook.

Curry powder is actually a pulverized blend of up to 20 spices, herbs and seeds. Among those most commonly used are cardamom, chiles, cinnamon, cloves, coriander, cumin, fennel seed, fenugreek, mace, nutmeg, red and black pepper, poppy and sesame seeds, saffron, tamarind and turmeric.

## Plan/Purchase

### Ingredients

| | |
|---|---|
| 1/4 | c. pine nuts |
| 1/4 | c. butter |
| 2 | lb. skinless, boneless chicken breast halves, cut into bite size pieces |
| 1 | onion, chopped |
| 4 | cloves garlic, minced |
| 2 | T. soy sauce |
| 14 | oz. unsweetened coconut milk |
| 1.5 | t. paprika |
| 1/4 | t. ground cumin |
| 1 | t. curry powder |
| 2 | t. cornstarch |
| 1/4 | c. cold water |

main dish    Plan · Purchase · Prep · Prepare · Plate · Present

# Saltimbocca with chicken

*Saltimbocca means to "jump in the mouth" in Italian, alluding to the fact that this dish is so good, it leaps into your mouth. This dish is relatively simple to make, as was the intention of the Romans who invented it. After a hard day of fighting the Visigoths, they wanted something that tasted good, and didn't require a lot of preparation (I assume that swinging a sword all day gets to be a bit tiring).*

*I've substituted chicken, for the traditional veal, and added a few other twists. The butter-sage sauce in the Sauce section finishes this dish off, and gives it a savory taste.*

## Plan/Purchase

### Ingredients

- **8**    **slices of Prosciutto, thinly sliced (Is there any other way, really?)**
- **4**    **boneless chicken breasts, pounded evenly... boom, boom, boom.**
- **1**    **bunch fresh baby spinach**
- **1**    **T. garlic, minced**
- **2**    **T. olive oil**
- **-**    **Salt and ground pepper (to taste)**

### Chef's Tip

*Since spinach, and other leafy plants, are typically grown in soil, make sure to thoroughly wash the spinach before using. As a matter a fact, a salad spinner is a good addition to any kitchen that uses a lot of leafy plants.*

~ 88 ~

## Prep/Prepare

1. Pound the chicken breasts to a 1/4-inch thickness. Incidentally, this is a great way to take out your frustrations (pretend the chicken is your boss, or in-laws) works every time.

2. Place 1 T. of oil and 2 T. of butter into a medium high heat skillet, & sauté the garlic until fragrant (about 2 minutes), then add the spinach & toss, using a pair of tongs, until wilted (about 3 minutes). Place the spinach into a covered bowl & & set aside. Don't wash the pan.

3. Lay a piece of pounded chicken onto a flat surface, & spread 1/4-cup of spinach across the chicken.

4. Take 2 T. of the cheese & sprinkle on top. This is where you can get a bit creative. I like the taste of pepper-jack or Swiss; however, you could go with Parmesan, traditional provolone, or whatever suits your tastes at that moment.

5. Roll the chicken breast up like a jelly roll, & then lay the breast, seam side down, to rest.

6. Lay two slices of Prosciutto side by side, lay the chicken breast at one end, & roll it up in the Prosciutto. Let it rest, seam side down. If you rolled the chicken breasts firmly, you won't need to use twine, or toothpicks to hold them together.

7. Repeat the process for the other 3 chicken breasts.

8. Place 1 T. of oil & 2 T. of butter into the hot pan (medium-high). When the butter stops foaming place the chicken, seam side down, into the pan. Use a pair of tongs (I love tongs) to turn the chicken & allow browning on all sides (about 6 to 8 minutes). Don't overcrowd the pan. It's possible you may have to do this in two batches.

9. Place the chicken on a rack (you want the heat to hit the chicken from all sides, so you want a rack. A cooling rack will do), set on a baking sheet, & cook in a pre-heated 400° f. oven for 5 minutes.

10. Let rest for 5 minutes.

## Plate/Present

*Sorry, ran out of room... be creative, and enjoy.*

*Cooking with a Plan Vol 1: Back to the Kitchen*     *main dish*

# Rotisserie Style Chicken

*I love rotisserie style chicken; however, unless you own a rotisserie, the only way to get good rotisserie chicken is at a restaurant (like Boston Market), or your local supermarket.*

*This recipe takes a bit of time (well, honestly, a LOT of time) and pre planning, but the results are great-tasting chicken infused with the flavors that only a rotisserie style chicken can deliver.*

*So, if you like great-tasting chicken, and you've got a bit of time on your hands, give this recipe a try.*

## Prep/Prepare

1. To create the rub, in a small bowl, mix together salt, paprika, onion powder, thyme, white pepper, black pepper, cayenne pepper, & garlic powder.
2. Remove and discard giblets from chicken. Rinse cavity, & pat dry with paper towel.
3. Rub the chicken inside & out with juice from the orange quarters. Then rub the chicken inside and out with the spice mixture, and place the orange quarters into the cavity of the chicken.
4. Cover the chicken, & refrigerate overnight, or at least 4 to 6 hours.
5. Place rack in the lower position of the oven, & then preheat to 250° f.
6. Place chicken in a roasting pan, & bake uncovered until the internal temperature reaches 180° f. (about 5 hours).
7. Let chicken rest (tented with foil) for 10 minutes before carving.

## Plate/Present

Carve the chicken starting with the breast. The chicken will be so tender, that removing the legs and thighs will be as simple as slicing through the skin, and gently pulling.

A recipe like this calls for a simple presentation with a side of garlic mash, and some corn, or possibly green beans (you decide).

It's also great for those late-night raids to the refrigerator... that is if there's anything left to save.

You might ask yourself why go to all this trouble, when you can get the dang chicken at a store, and probably not pay much more for it... Good Question.

Here's my answer: **CONTROL**. When you're making the chicken, you can control the ingredients in the rub; even what you cook inside the bird. For example, I like more pepper, less garlic powder, and occasionally I use an onion in the cavity, as opposed to an orange... I like control.

## Plan/Purchase

### Ingredients

| | |
|---|---|
| 1 | t. salt |
| 1 | t. paprika |
| 1/2 | t. onion powder |
| 1/2 | t. dried thyme |
| 1/2 | t. white pepper |
| 1/4 | t. cayenne pepper |
| 1/4 | t. black pepper |
| 1/4 | t. garlic powder |
| 1 | orange, quartered |
| 1 | (4 lb) whole chicken |

### Important

*When handling raw chicken, wash your hands often in hot soapy water. This helps prevent cross-contamination of all those nasty little critters that like to inhabit raw chicken.*

### Oven Accuracy

*It's important to rely solely on the internal temperature of the chicken, and not an arbitrary time.*

main dish | Plan · Purchase · Prep · Prepare · Plate · Present

# Mouth Watering Cilantro Chicken

*This is one of my all-time favorite recipes, and of my guests (if you count the number of times it gets requested at gatherings). This is an easy recipe to prepare; taking a little over an hour from prep to table.*

*The tang of the vinegar and soy (you can use low sodium, if you want) are offset by the sweetness of the sugar, and cooking for an hour with the chilies and ginger (not to mention the chicken), gives this sauce a mellow flavor, that will have your guests wanting more... I promise.*

## Plan/Purchase

### Ingredients

| | |
|---|---|
| 3 | lb. chicken (2 thighs, 2 breasts) |
| 3 | jalapeno chillies, seeded and small diced |
| 1 | T. ginger, grated |
| 2 | c water |
| 1/2 | c. white wine vinegar |
| 2/3 | c. soy sauce |
| 2/3 | c. sugar |
| 1/2 | c. cilantro, rough chopped, reserve a few leaves for decorating the plate |

### Jalapeno

*A small green chile pepper that is mildly hot. They are named after Jalapa, the capital of Veracruz.*

### What the Recipe Doesn't Know

**The type of pan you're using.**

*The pan should be large enough to easily hold the chicken pieces (don't crowd), and deep enough to hold the ingredients for the sauce without spilling over while the sauce is simmering.*

## Prep/Prepare

1. Combine water, white wine vinegar, soy sauce, & sugar in a deep pan, & then bring to a slow simmer.
2. After sugar dissolves, add ginger and chillies, & simmer for 3 minutes
3. Add chicken, cover and simmer for 30 minutes. Turn chicken twice, during this step.
4. Remove lid and continue to simmer, turning chicken until it reduces & thickens to the consistency of maple syrup, (15 to 25 minutes).
5. Remove chicken from pan, cover & keep warm.
6. Pour sauce into a fat separator to remove the grease, & then return to pan.
7. Stir in the cilantro.
8. Return chicken to pan, and turn to thoroughly cover with the sauce.

## Plate/Present

Place about 1/2 cup of steamed rice in a loose mound on one side of the plate, and then lay a piece of chicken, half on, half off the rice mound... put some veggies on the other side of the plate. Drizzle the sauce over the chicken and rice, and toss a few cilantro leaves over the plate for decoration.

Or... once the chicken cools slightly, remove the skin and then use your hands to tear the chicken into rough strips. Place the chicken on a plate side-by-side with the rice, and place the sauce into small individual dipping bowls (veggies an option on this one).

On a dinner table using southwestern decor. You might want to finish it off with margaritas on the patio.

## Chef's Tip

Remember this is all about a slow simmer (the operative word being, slow). If you try to rush this dish by raising the temperature of the pan, you'll only succeed in burning the sauce... And I hate it when that happens.

Cooking with a Plan Vol I: Back to the Kitchen          main dish

# Chicken Cordon Bleu

*Most people have a tendency to stay away from recipes that they can't pronounce. They like to eat them, but assume they're too hard to prepare. This recipe has great taste, is easy to make, and that's a good thing.*

*Chicken breasts are carefully pounded until thin, and then wrapped with cheese and ham. Finally, they're coated with fresh bread crumbs and cooked, for a one-of-a-kind taste.*

*Give this one a try, and I think that you'll like it... I certainly do.*

## Prep/Prepare

1. Place a rack in the middle position of your oven, & preheat to 350° f.
2. Coat a baking dish with nonstick cooking spray,
3. Pound the chicken breasts to 1/4 inch thickness (see Appendix A: Pounding Cuts of Meat).
4. In a small dish blend the egg with a tablespoon of water, dip the chicken in the egg wash, & lay on a piece of parchment paper.
5. Sprinkle the chicken pieces on both sides with salt & pepper.
6. Place a piece of cheese & ham on top of each breast.
7. Roll up each breast, & secure with a toothpick or cooking twine. Place in baking dish, & sprinkle chicken evenly with bread crumbs.
8. Bake for 45 to 50 minutes, or until juices run clear. Internal temperature of chicken should reach 165° f.
9. Remove from oven, place a cheese slice on top of each breast, and then return to the oven for 3 to 5 more minutes, cheese should be melted.

## Plate/Present

Word of caution: The filling will be hot and may splatter; let stand approximately 5 minutes to cool before serving.

Remove the toothpicks, or twine from the chicken, and use a sharp knife to cut into medium slices (1/2 to 3/4 of an inch).

Then plate with your favorite veggies, or some garlic mashed potatoes.

## Plan/Purchase

### Ingredients

| | |
|---|---|
| 4 | skinless, boneless chicken breast halves |
| 1/4 | t. salt |
| 1/8 | t. ground black pepper |
| 8 | slices Swiss cheese |
| 4 | slices cooked ham |
| 1/2 | c. seasoned bread crumbs |
| 1 | egg |

### For Your Information

*The words cordon bleu are French for blue ribbon, and they referred to a blue sash worn by senior students at the Institute de Saint-Louis, founded in 1686 for the daughters of impoverished nobility.*

main dish — Plan · Purchase · Prep · Prepare · Plate · Present

# Pasta & Chicken with a creamy parmesan sauce

Pasta is a universally enjoyed food, and almost every country serves some type of noodle dish. In China, it is mein; Japan, udon; Poland, pierogi; Germany, spaetzle. The popularity of pasta can be attributed to several factors: it is easily manufactured, it takes up little storage space, keeps for a long time, and is easy to cook.

All I can say is that I love pasta dishes, and growing up with an Italian aunt might explain why. This particular dish is simple to make and packs a lot of homey taste.

## Plan/Purchase

**Pasta**

| | |
|---|---|
| 4 | oz. angel-hair pasta |
| 1 | c. arugula leaves, torn |

**Sauce**

| | |
|---|---|
| 3 | T. heavy cream |
| 2 | T. parmesan cheese, grated |
| 1 | egg yolk * |
| 1 | t. lemon zest |
| - | salt & pepper, to taste |
| 1 | pinch, red pepper flakes |

**Chicken**

| | |
|---|---|
| 2 | chicken breasts |
| - | salt/pepper, to taste |
| 2 | T. butter |
| 2 | T. olive oil |

### For Your Information

This recipe uses raw eggs as one of the ingredients in the sauce. Raw eggs have been a known source of salmonella (I bet that got your attention), and therefore should be used carefully. See Appendix A: Use of Raw Egg Products for more information on this subject.

~ 92 ~

## Prep/Prepare

1. Whisk all ingredients for the sauce in a non-reactive bowl.
2. Store the sauce (covered) in the refrigerator.
3. Brine the chicken (see appendix A: Brinning), for 1 hour.
4. Remove chicken from brine, rinse & pat dry.
5. Cut chicken into 1 inch strips, & season with salt and pepper.
6. Add oil & butter in a medium saute pan over high heat, until foaming subsides.
7. Saute chicken strips until browned on all sides.
8. Cook the pasta according to package directions, until al dente.

## Plate/Present

Place the pasta into a large bowl while still steaming hot, and then use a pair of tongs to lightly toss the torn arugula leaves until slightly wilted. Add the Parmesan sauce, and use the tongs to lightly coat the pasta.

Place the chicken strips on top, and serve family style.

Or, you could place a helping of the pasta on individual plates, and then place a few chicken strips on top.

I've always preferred to plate pasta using plain white dishes, and pair it with a good white wine (Chardonnay, Riesling).

To make this dish even simpler, you could eliminate the chicken, and just go with the pasta and sauce. The bite of the arugula, makes for a very flavorful dish, even without the chicken.

Don't forget to have some freshly grated Parmesan, salt, pepper, and maybe some red pepper flakes (for the adventurous).

Oh, and don't forget that crusty loaf of bread.

*Cooking with a Plan Vol 1: Back to the Kitchen*     main dish

# Chicken Piccata

*Piccata translates to piquant or piquancy, which means tart or zesty. Chicken piccata does have a tart sauce, and the traditional additions of lemon juice, white wine and capers, help to make that happen.*

*The sauce is finished by cutting 3 tablespoons of cold butter into cubes, and whisking into the pan sauce... 1 tablespoon at a time. Remember to let the butter completely melt into the sauce before adding another tablespoon, or you could break the sauce.*

## Prep/Prepare

1. Take one lemon & thinly slice,
2. Juice the other two lemons to produce 1/4 cup of juice.
3. Slice each chicken breast in half, horizontally. This will produce 8 breast halves approximately 1/2 inch thick.
4. Sprinkle chicken with salt & pepper.
5. Put flour into a shallow dish, & coat breasts completely.
6. In a 12-inch skillet over medium-high heat add 2 tablespoons of oil.
7. Sauté half the chicken, until lightly browned on first side (2 to 2 1/2 minutes). Turn & cook 2 1/2 minutes longer, or until lightly brown on second side.
8. Repeat for remaining cutlets.
9. Add shallot to the empty skillet. Heat skillet over medium heat, & sauté until fragrant (30 seconds).
10. Add the stock & sliced lemon to the skillet, over high heat, & then use a wooden spoon to scrape up the brown bits (called fonds).
11. Continue to simmer until 1/3 cup of liquid remains (4 to 6 minutes).
12. Add the capers & lemon juice, then simmer until sauce reduces back to 1/3 cup (1 to 3 minutes).
13. Remove from heat and incorporate butter to thicken the sauce;
14. As a final step add the parsley.

## Plate/Present

Remove the chicken from the oven, place two cutlets on a plate, and spoon sauce over chicken. It's usually served with polenta, or some pasta.

## Plan/Purchase

### Ingredients

| | |
|---|---|
| 3 | large lemons |
| 4 | boneless, skinless chicken breasts |
| - | salt and pepper, to taste |
| 1/2 | c. all-purpose flour |
| 4 | T. vegetable or grape seed oil |
| 1 | shallot, minced |
| 1 | c. chicken stock or broth, canned or homemade |
| 2 | T. small capers, drained |
| 3 | T. unsalted butter, room temperature |
| 2 | T. fresh parsley, minced |

### Preperation Tip

*To cut the chicken breasts in half, lay them on a firm surface, lay your hand on top, and using a sharp knife, cut them in half.*

### Chef's Tip

*To keep the sautéd chicken breasts from cooling off, preheat an oven to 200° f. and then place the first batch, of chicken on a covered plate, in the warm oven.*

main dish — Plan - Purchase - Prep - Prepare - Plate - Present

# Garlic Chicken

*If you like garlic, then you're going to love this recipe. The chicken comes out tender and moist, and is loaded with flavor... and not just garlic flavor. Actually, the garlic helps to bring out a medley of flavors from the baking chicken.*

*The sides for this one vary. For example, if you want to go heavy, go with some mash potatoes; however, if you want it a bit lighter, then steam up some rice. A good veggie would be carrots or green beans.*

## Plan/Purchase

### Ingredients

| | |
|---|---|
| 1 | egg yolk |
| 6 | cloves garlic, chopped |
| 4 | skinless, boneless chicken breast halves |
| 6 | T. butter, melted |
| 1 | c. dry bread crumbs |
| 1 | c. grated Parmesan cheese |
| 1 | T. dried parsley |
| 1 | T. garlic powder |
| 1/2 | T. salt |
| 1 | T. ground black pepper |

### Chef's Tip

*Instead of using a bowl, you could always put the garlic/egg mixture into a large zip lock bag. You can then massage the bag occasionally to distribute the marinade.*

### For Your Information

*The bulb of Allium sativum (garlic) has a pungent odor when crushed, and is widely used to flavor foods. There is some evidence that garlic has a beneficial effect in lowering blood cholesterol.*

## Prep/Prepare

1. Mix egg yolk with garlic, in a bowl.
2. Place chicken in egg mixture, and turn to coat. Cover dish and refrigerate for at least 4 hours, or overnight if possible.
3. Adjust rack to the middle position in your oven, and then preheat to 400° f.
4. Line a 9x13 inch baking dish with parchment paper, and then add the melted butter.
5. Mix bread crumbs, cheese, parsley, garlic powder, salt and pepper in a shallow bowl, and use mixture to thoroughly coat the chicken.
6. Place chicken into the baking dish, and as a final step before baking, pour remaining egg mixture over the top
7. Bake for 15 to 20 minutes on each side, or until juices run clear. Internal temperature of chicken should reach 170° f.

## Plate/Present

Let the chicken rest for 3 to 5 minutes. Then take a chicken breast and slice it on the diagonal. Lay the slices right on top of a mound of mash potatoes... If you're really into garlic, you could make some garlic mash. Some sliced green beans complete the scene and make for a colorful, and very tasty dish.

~ 94 ~

Cooking with a Plan Vol 1: Back to the Kitchen — main dish

# Sesame & Teriyaki Chicken Wings

*Sorry, as much as I love chicken wings, I just had to put in a recipe for a variation on these classic bites. Technically, this would probably go under the category of an appetizer, however, they can also make a lunch, or late night (reheated) snack. This particular recipe is not the traditional wings created in Buffalo, New York; the sauce is a combination of teriyaki and sesame. But if you're a wings lover, I've included the recipe for the sauce used on traditional wings.*

*So, step up to the bar, grab your favorite larger, and take a bite out of these beauties.*

## Prep/Prepare

1. In a large bowl combine teriyaki sauces, soy sauce, honey, vinegar, sesame oil, garlic & cayenne pepper.
2. Add the chicken wings, cover & marinate overnight in the refrigerator. Don't skip this step... it's important.
3. Remove chicken wings from the marinade, sprinkle with toasted sesame seeds, and then place on a foil lined baking sheet.
4. Bake at 425° for 30 minutes or until juices run clear.
5. Remove from oven and allow to cool for 3 to five minutes.

## Plate/Present

Serve on a platter lined with salad greens, and a lot of napkins.

## Additions

The original Buffalo wings sauce is actually quite simple: 1 cup Franks Red Hot Sauce, 1/3 cup butter, and 1/4 cup apple cider vinegar. Let the wings soak for a few minutes, and then deep fry.

These wings can be made 1 day ahead, if stored in the refrigerator. Just heat up in the microwave slightly before serving, or pop them into a 275° f. oven for about 15 minutes.

## Plan/Purchase

### Ingredients

| | | |
|---|---|---|
| 1.5 | lb. | chicken wings |
| 2 | T. | teriyaki stir fry sauce |
| 2 | T. | teriyaki marinade and sauce |
| 3 | T. | soy sauce |
| 1 | T. | honey |
| 1 | T. | white vinegar |
| 2 | t. | toasted sesame oil |
| 1 | | garlic clove, minced |
| 1/4 | t. | cayenne pepper |
| 2 | T. | Toasted sesame seeds |

### For Your Information

History says, that the first buffalo wings were prepared at the Anchor Bar located at 1047 Main Street, between North Street and Summer Street in, Buffalo, New York, on October 3, 1964, by Teressa Bellissimo, co-owner of the Anchor Bar with her husband Frank.

#  Fish

Any of numerous cold-blooded aquatic vertebrates of the superclass Pisces, characteristically having fins, gills, and a streamlined body and including specifically:

- Any of the class Osteichthyes, having a bony skeleton.
- Any of the class Chondrichthyes, having a cartilaginous skeleton and including the sharks, rays, and skates.
- The flesh of such animals used as food.
- Any of various primitive aquatic vertebrates of the class Cyclostomata, lacking jaws and including the lampreys and hagfishes.

The definition of fish can be considered one of more than 24,000 species of cold-blooded vertebrates found worldwide in fresh and salt water. Living species range from the primitive lampreys and hagfishes through the cartilaginous sharks, skates, and rays to the abundant and diverse bony fishes. Species range in length from 0.4 in. (10 mm) to more than 60 ft (20 m).

The body is generally tapered at both ends. Most species that inhabit surface or mid-water regions are streamlined or are flattened side to side; most bottom dwellers are flattened top to bottom. Tropical species are often brightly colored. Most species have paired fins and skin covered with either bony or toothlike scales. Fish generally respire through gills. Most bony fishes have a swim bladder, a gas-filled organ used to adjust swimming depth. Most species lay eggs, which may be fertilized externally or internally. Fishes first appeared more than 450 million years ago.

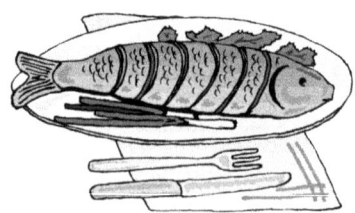

# The Deep Blue Sea

*main dish*  Plan · Purchase · Prep · Prepare · Plate · Present

# Drunken Salmon with thyme and red pepper cream

Okay, this cookbook contains a recipe for drunken pot roast, so why not get the fish drunk. This dish uses a sake marinade to flavor the salmon, and a pineapple reduction conveniently located in the section on sauces.

Salmon is considered a large game fish, typically found in cold northern waters. It has a delicate pinkish flesh and swims from salt to fresh water to spawn.

## Plan/Purchase

### Ingredients

| | |
|---|---|
| 1 | (10-oz.) salmon fillet |
| 1 | T. chopped fresh ginger |
| 2 | cloves garlic, finely chopped |
| 1 | finely chopped scallion |
| - | salt and freshly ground black pepper, to taste |
| 1 | c. medium to dry sake |
| 2 | c. cooked white or brown rice |

### For Your Information

Pacific salmon may be a source of vitamin A and a rich source of vitamin D; canned salmon, in which the softened bones are edible, is also a source of calcium.

So, dig in... because it tastes great, and it's good for you.

## Prep/Prepare

1. Place the salmon in a nice deep bowl.
2. Add the ginger, garlic, scallions, salt, & pepper.
3. Cover with sake, & let stand for 2 hours, in the refrigerator.
4. Place the salmon on a medium-hot grill (see Appendix A: Techniques Grilling Temperature).
5. Remove salmon from marinade and lightly season with salt & pepper.
6. Cook about 3 minutes per side.

## Plate/Present

Presentation of this dish can go in two directions: fancy or rustic. In the fancy version, you would place a small mound of rice in the middle of a stark white plate, place the salmon on top and then drizzle with the pineapple reduction (you have to try the sauce, it's fantastic).

In the rustic version, you place all the salmon on one plate, along with a large bowl of rice, and another for the pineapple reduction. Then set out some plates, forks, etc, and let your guests have at it.

After all it's salmon on a BBQ, and traditionally BBQ's have a casual air to them... at least that's what I've been brought up to believe.

Cooking with a Plan Vol 1: Back to the Kitchen  main dish

# East Coast Crab Cakes Pan Fried

*I love crabcakes... let me say that again... I LOVE crabcakes. Unfortunately, good ones are hard to come by; especially, when you live in land-locked Kansas. So, whenever I travel to the East Coast, you'll find me nosing around the waterfront, looking for that elusive great-tasting crab cake... It's a hard job, but somebody has to do it.*

*I'm not promising that this recipe will make you think you're in Maine; however, when you take a bite, don't be surprised if you get a whiff of salt air, and hear the sound of seagulls, plying the coast... Oh to be in Maine, when the crabs are harvested.*

## Prep/Prepare

1. To make the dipping sauce: Mix all ingredients in a small bowl, then cover & refrigerate until flavors blend, about 30 minutes.
2. Gently mix crab meat, scallions, herb, Old Bay, bread crumbs, and mayonnaise in medium bowl, being careful not to break up the crab lumps.
3. Season with salt & white pepper, to taste.
4. Carefully fold in egg with a rubber spatula until mixture just clings together.
5. Divide crab mixture into four portions & shape each into a round cake, about 3 inches across and 1 1/2-inches high.
6. Arrange on baking sheet lined with parchment paper; cover with plastic wrap & chill at least 30 minutes. (or up to 24 hours.)
7. Put flour on plate or in pie tin.
8. Lightly dredge crab cakes though the flour until thoroughly coated.
9. Heat oil in large, skillet over medium-high heat until hot but not smoking.
10. Gently lay chilled crab cakes in skillet, and-fry until the outsides are crisp and browned, abour 4 to 5 minutes per side.

## Plate/Present

Take a white porcelain plate, sprinkle with some dry thyme, place several spoonfuls of the dipping sauce in the middle and spread into a circle. Place the hot crab cake in the middle (right on the sauce) and then lay two of the lemon wedges on either side of the cake.

If you want to go crazy, deep fry some Japanese rice noodles, and place a bunch on top of the crab cake... like I said: Crazy.

## Plan/Purchase

### Crab Cakes

| | |
|---|---|
| 1 | lb. lump crabmeat (preferably jumbo lump), picked over to remove cartilage and shell fragments |
| 4 | medium scallions, green part only, minced (about 1/2 cup) |
| 1 | T. fresh dill, or basil, chopped |
| 1 1/2 | t. Old Bay seasoning |
| 2 | T. dry bread crumbs |
| 1/4 | c. mayonnaise |
| - | salt and pepper, to taste |
| 1 | large egg |
| 1/4 | c. unbleached all-purpose flour |
| 4 | T. vegetable oil |
| 2 | lemons, cut into wedges |

### Dipping Sauce

| | |
|---|---|
| 1/4 c. | mayonnaise |
| 1/4 c. | sour cream |
| 2 | t. canned chipotle pepper in adobo sauce, minced |
| 1 | small clove of garlic, minced |
| 2 | t. fresh cilantro leaf, minced |
| 1 | t. lime juice from 1 small lime |

~ 99 ~

main dish    Plan - Purchase - Prep - Prepare - Plate - Present

# Baked Fish south of the border style

*This is an easy-to-make dish, and the cool news is that you get to choose how hot you want it... if you're a wimp, choose a mild salsa... of if you want to live on the wild size, choose a salsa with some fire in it. It's totally up to you, and your guests.*

*You want to use a good firm white fish like cod for this recipe; however, their's nothing to say that you can't experiment with other fish, or even a combination of fish. Heck, throw in some scallops, if you're feeling adventurous.*

## Plan/Purchase

### Ingredients

- 1 1/2 lb. cod
- 1 c. salsa (your choice)
- 1 c. shredded cheddar cheese (preferably sharp)
- 1/2 c. coarsely crushed corn chips
- 1 avocado peeled, pitted and sliced
- 1/4 c. sour cream

### Cooking Tip

It is easy to tell when seafood is done by the way it looks...it turns opaque and flakes easy with a fork. When done, the internal temperature of the fish on a cooking thermometer should be 145°F.

### For Your Information

There are more than 24,000 species of cold-blooded vertebrates found worldwide in fresh and salt water. Can you name them all?

## Prep/Prep

1. Preheat your oven to 400° f.
2. Put some olive oil, or melted butter on a paper towel, & grease the inside of an 8x12 baking dish.
3. Rinse the fish fillets in cold water, & then pat dry with paper towels.
4. Lay fillets side by side in the baking dish, pour the salsa over the top, & sprinkle the top with the shredded cheese. Top with the crushed corn chips.
5. Bake, uncovered, until fish is opaque & flakes with a fork about 15 to 20 minutes.

## Plate/Present

Leave the dish rustic and bring it to the table in its baking dish. Take care to protect the table (a trivet). Have a couple of spatulas handy so that you guests can grab their share.

Since this is south of the border fare, it must be served with sliced avocado and sour cream... on the side, of course.

And, how about a pitcher of margaritas? Now, let's have a party.

## Chef's Tip

Another good thing about this recipe is that it's low-cal, and its good for you. But don't let that fool you, it's bursting with great flavors

*Cooking with a Plan Vol 1: Back to the Kitchen*  *main dish*

# Fish Tacos

*If you've never tried fish tacos, then what are you waiting for... This recipe is packed with great taste, and it's healthy for you... well, almost.*

*This recipe has three stages: making the beer batter (that's right, beer), making the white sauce, and finally baking the fish. If you're in a crunch, you can always make the batter ahead of time; cover and refrigerate, and bring out when needed.*

## Prep/Prepare

1. Combine flour, cornstarch, baking powder, & salt in a large bowl. Blend egg & beer, then quickly stir into the flour mixture until smooth. Set aside.
2. Mix together yogurt and mayonnaise in a small bowl. Stir in fresh lime juice until smooth and slightly thin. Incorporate the jalapeno, capers, oregano, cumin, dill, & cayenne, & then set aside.
3. Dust fish pieces lightly with flour.
4. Dip into beer batter, & fry until crisp & golden brown, and then drain on paper towels.

## Plate/Present

To serve, place fried fish in a tortilla, and top with shredded cabbage, and white sauce.

## Tortilla Warming Trick

A great trick here is to take a tea towel, and make it just damp. Before warming the tortillas in the oven, cover with the towel. The slight amount of water in the towel will help to keep the tortillas fresh and warm.

## Plan/Purchase

### Beer Batter

| | |
|---|---|
| 1 | c. all-purpose flour |
| 2 | T. cornstarch |
| 1 | t. baking powder |
| 1/2 | t. salt |
| 1 | egg |
| 1 | c. beer |

### White Sauce

| | |
|---|---|
| 1/2 | c. plain yogurt |
| 1/2 | c. mayonnaise |
| 1 | lime, juiced |
| 1 | jalapeno pepper, minced |
| 1 | t. minced capers |
| 1/2 | t. dried oregano |
| 1/2 | t. ground cumin |
| 1/2 | t. dried dill weed |
| 1 | t. ground cayenne pepper |

### Fish

| | |
|---|---|
| 1 | qt. oil for frying |
| 1 | lb. cod fillets, cut into 2 to 3 oz. portions |
| 1 | (12 oz.) package soft flour tortillas |
| 1/2 | medium head cabbage, finely shredded |

~ 101 ~

main dish — Plan · Purchase · Prep · Prepare · Plate · Present

# Fish Meuniere *with toasted slivered almonds*

Meuniere [muhn-YEHR] (French for miller's wife) refers to the cooking technique of lightly dusting meat, fish or poultry with flour before sautéing.

Maitre d'Hotel butter is butter combined with lemon juice and parsley. Rather than melting the butter and adding the lemon juice and parsley, the butter is kneaded with the lemon juice and parsley. Solid pieces of this mixture are then placed on the hot meat, fish or poultry and allowed to melt. Or, if you don't want to go the trouble, you might want to try browned butter, as this recipe suggests.

## Plan/Purchase

### Fish Meuniere

| | |
|---|---|
| 1/2 | c. unbleached all-purpose flour |
| 4 | sole or flounder fillets, 5 to 6 oz each and 3/8 inch thick, patted dry |
| - | table salt and ground black pepper, to taste |
| 2 | T. vegetable oil |
| 2 | T. unsalted butter, cut into 2 pieces |
| 1 | lemon, cut in wedges for serving |

### Maitre d'Hotel butter

| | |
|---|---|
| 4 | T. unsalted butter, cut into 4 pieces |
| 1/4 | c. slivered almonds |
| 1 | T. chopped fresh parsley leaves |
| 1 1/2 | T. fresh lemon juice |

### Maitre d'Hotel Butter

*This should not be confused with "beurre manie" (kneaded butter), which is equal parts of flour, and butter kneaded together and used to thicken sauces.*

### Chef's Tip

*Adjust oven rack to lower-middle position, set 4 heat proof dinner plates on rack, and heat oven to 200 degrees. These pre-heated plates will help to keep the fish warm for your guests.*

## Prep/Prepare

*Fish Meuniere*

1. Place flour in large baking dish. Season both sides of each fillet generously with salt & pepper; let fillets stand, about 5 minutes.
2. Lightly coat both sides of fillets with flour, & place in single layer on a parchment-lined baking sheet.
3. Place 1 T. oil in 12-inch nonstick skillet over high heat until shimmering, then add 1 T. butter & swirl to coat pan bottom; when foaming subsides, carefully place 2 fillets in skillet, bone-side down.
4. Reduce heat to medium-high and cook, without moving fish, until edges of fillets are opaque and bottom is golden brown, about 3 minutes.
5. Gently flip fillets & cook on second side until thickest part of fillet easily separates into flakes, about 2 minutes longer.
6. Transfer fillets, to dinner plates, & return plates to oven.
7. Repeat for remaining fish.

*Browned Butter*

8. Heat butter in 10-inch skillet over medium-high heat until butter melts, 1 to 1 1/2 minutes.
9. Add almonds and continue to cook, swirling pan constantly, until butter is golden brown & has a nutty aroma.
10. Remove skillet from heat.

## Plate/Present

Remove plates from oven (see Chef's Tip) and sprinkle fillets with parsley. Add lemon juice to browned butter and season to taste with salt; spoon sauce over fish and serve immediately with lemon wedges.

This dish goes well with a good long-grain rice, and a green veggie, like broccoli.

Cooking with a Plan Vol I: Back to the Kitchen  main dish

# Grilled Tilapia

*[tuh-LAH-pee-uh] has been an important food fish in Africa for eons. Tilapia are farmed around the world from Asia, to South America, to the United States and Canada. The lowfat flesh is white (sometimes tinged with pink), sweet and fine-textured. It's suitable for baking, broiling, grilling and steaming.*

*Tilapia is also called St. Peter's fish because legend says that this is the fish Jesus used to feed the multitude.*

## Prep/Prepare

1. Combine all the ingredients for the cashew yogurt sauce in a small bowl, then cover and refrigerate until needed.
2. Preheat & clean your grill. (See Appendix B: Cleaning your grill).
3. Cut the fillet in half lengthwise. Lightly season the fish with the cumin, cayenne, paprika, and salt.
4. Coat each piece in olive oil and grill, 3 to 4 minutes on each side.

## Plate/Present

Begin by covering a dinner plate with a layer of cashew yogurt sauce. Place the pieces of grilled tilapia in the center, overlapping one another. .

## Plan/Purchase

### Fish

| | |
|---|---|
| 6 | oz. tilapia fillet |
| 1/4 | t. ground cumin |
| 1/4 | t. cayenne pepper |
| 1/4 | t. paprika |
| 1/4 | t. kosher salt |
| 1 | T. olive oil |

### Cashew Yogurt Sauce

| | |
|---|---|
| 1/4 | c. mayonnaise |
| 1/4 | c. sour cream |
| 2 | t. chipotle pepper in adobo sauce, minced |
| 1 | small clove of garlic, minced |
| 2 | t. fresh cilantro leaf, minced |
| 1 | t. lime juice |

### Chef;s Tip

*Fish is best cooked quickly over high heat. Remember the 10 minute rule: For every inch of thickness, cook for 10 minutes.*

main dish  Plan · Purchase · Prep · Prepare · Plate · Present

# Cilantro and Tomato Seafood Bake

*What's better on a cool autumn evening then a warm bowl, chock full of the sea's bounty. When selecting the fish, go to your fishmonger and go with fresh, and try to avoid, if you can, frozen.*

*Canned Italian tomatoes are acceptable, but fresh vegetables from a local farmer's market are always the best bet. The trouble is, it's hard to get fresh veggies in the Fall or Winter… do your best… I'm counting on you (and so are your guests).*

## Plan/Purchase

### Ingredients

| | |
|---|---|
| 1 | t. olive oil |
| 1 | t. chopped fresh ginger |
| 1/2 | c. chopped leeks |
| 2 | stalks chopped celery |
| 1/2 | c. white wine |
| 12 | oz. chopped tomatoes |
| 1/2 | c. chopped fresh cilantro |
| 10 | oz. firm whitefish, cut into 1/2 inch slices |
| 8 | large shrimp (16-20 count) |
| 8 | good size scallops |
| 2 | T. grated Parmesan |
| 1/2 | c. sliced mushrooms |

### Fresh Fish

When selecting your fish, take a nice big sniff… the fish should not smell like fish… it should smell fresh like the ocean… that's fresh fish.

### Whitefish

Whitefish is a fisheries term referring to several species of oceanic deep water fish particularly cod, whiting, and haddock, but also hake, pollock, or others.

~ 104 ~

## Prep/Prepare

1. Place rack in the middle position, & preheat the oven to 325° f.
2. Heat oil in frying pan over medium heat, & then sauté ginger, leek, & celery for about 2 to 3 minutes.
3. Add the wine & tomatoes, & then bring to a slow boil.
4. Stir in the cilantro, & remove from heat.
5. Place fish, scallops, & shrimp into casserole dish, & then pour tomato mixture over the fish.
6. Bake for 10 to 15 minutes (fish flakes, but is still slightly pink on the inside).

## Plate/Present

This dish can be cooked and served in the same pan: ovenproof glass bake ware is ideal for this recipe.

You could add some steamed rice; however, this dish will stand on its own.

*Cooking with a Plan Vol 1: Back to the Kitchen*     *main dish*

# Spicy Fish Cakes

*Okay, you like crab cakes; however, you can't always get good crab (I'm from Kansas, tell me about it), or you just don't want to go to the added expense of good crab... but you like crab cakes.*

*While I'm not saying these fish cakes will fool you into thinking you're eating crab; however, they are a great alternative. And, just because they're inexpensive to make, doesn't mean they're not loaded with great flavor.*

*Give them a try, and I think that you will agree.*

## Prep/Prepare

1. Preheat oven to 375F
2. Place white fish on a baking sheet lined with parchment paper, and bake for 15 minutes.
3. Let cool, and flake the fish into the bowl of a food processor fitted with a steel blade, (make sure there are no remaining bones).
4. Add eggs to the white fish, and then process into a course paste... set aside.
5. Take 1 cup bread crumbs, season with pepper and cayenne, and set aside.
6. Combine the remainder of the ingredients (minus oil and bread crumbs) in a small bowl.
7. Use a wooden spoon to incorporate the ingredients with the egg/fish mixture.
8. Add the breadcrumbs (do not over mix).
9. Shape into 4 large fish cakes, and roll in the spiced bread crumbs. Place the cakes in the refrigerator for 30 minutes.
10. Heat oil in a medium-high heat pan, and cook fish cakes 1 to 2 minutes on each side.
11. Place cakes on a baking sheet lined with parchment paper, and bake for about 8 minutes.

## Plate/Present

Place a small bed of shredded lettuce in the middle of a plate, and cover with a tablespoon of dipping sauce of your choice. Place the fish cake on top of the salad, and decorate the plate with more of the sauce.

## Plan/Purchase

### Crab Cakes

| | |
|---|---|
| 1 | lb. white fish |
| 2 | eggs |
| 2 | c. fresh breadcrumbs |
| | ground black pepper, to taste |
| - | cayenne pepper, to taste |
| 1 | T. mayonnaise |
| 2 | t. Dijon mustard |
| 1 | T. fresh thyme, chopped |
| 1/4 | c. fresh parsley, chopped |
| 1 | T. paprika |
| 1/2 | yellow onion, diced |
| 1/2 | C. celery, chopped |
| 2 | t. Worcestershire sauce |
| | Tabasco sauce, to taste |
| 1/2 | lime, juice and zest |
| 2 | t. olive oil |

### Chef's Tip

*If you want a sauce, you can always use the same dipping sauce as prepared for the crab cakes.*

~ 105 ~

main dish     Plan · Purchase · Prep · Prepare · Plate · Present

# Pan Roasted Halibut

*Pan roasting fish, brings a lot of flavor to the halibut; however, the high heat can make for a smoky kitchen. One tip is to use a high smoke point oil, like grapeseed oil. Another is to make sure you have a good hood over your range to help suck up the smoke.*

*If you've got all that covered, then you can get to work. As you can see, the ingredients are few, so it's all up to the fish. In this case, halibut has a deep flavor that works with almost anything. Make sure the fish is fresh (it should smell like the ocean).*

## Plan/Purchase

### Ingredients

- 2    T. olive oil
- 2    halibut steaks
- -    Salt and ground black pepper, to taste

### Cooking Tip

The halibut steaks should be 1 & 1/4 inches thick and 10 to 12 inches long, rinsed, dried well with paper towels, and trimmed of cartilage at both ends.

### Chef's Tip

Avoid fish that smells "fishy".

In addition, there's really not any need for a sauce with this dish. Believe me, the fish will stand on its own... truth.

## Prep/Prepare

1. Adjust rack to middle position in the oven, and heat to 425° f.
2. Heat. oil in 12-inch, ovenproof skillet over high heat (oil should begin to smoke).
3. Lightly coat the halibut steaks with salt and pepper.
4. Reduce heat to medium-high, and lay steaks in pan and sear, without moving, until spotty brown, about 4 minutes
5. Take pan off the heat.
6. Carefully flip steaks over.
7. Transfer skillet to oven and bake for about 10 minutes, or until fish begins to flake.

## Plate/Present

Place a bed of steamed rice, and broccoli on a pre-warmed plate, and then place a piece of the halibut over the rice. Serve immediately.

Cooking with a Plan Vol I: Back to the Kitchen — main dish

# Baked Salmon

*If you like salmon, but you've been a bit hesitant about trying some of the more exotic methods, like planking on a grill (there's even a recipe for salmon that includes using your dishwasher, but I won't go there), then this just might be your perfect recipe. It's simple, but packed with great flavor. Try it once, and I'll bet you'll be trying it again and again. This recipe requires a bit of prep (the marinade); however, like any great chef, you've included that in your time line… right?*

*Then, when you're brave enough, you just might want to try your dishwasher… don't ask.*

## Prep/Prepare

1. Fix the marinade by mixing the garlic, olive oil, basil, salt, pepper, lemon juice and parsley in a small non-reactive bowl.
2. Place salmon fillets in a glass baking dish, and cover with the marinade.
3. Cover and place in the refrigerator 1 to 2 hours, turn several times.
4. Place a rack in the middle position of the oven, and preheat to 375° f.
5. Remove salmon from refrigerator, place two slices of lemon on top of each fillet, and then cover the baking dish with foil
6. Bake 35 to 45 minutes, until easily flaked with a fork.

## Plate/Present

Place a mound of rice on a pre-warmed plate and put one of the salmon fillets right on top. Then drizzle with the marinade. Repeat for the second fillet.

Place a few of the remaining lemon slices on the plate, and serve immediately.

## Plan/Purchase

### Ingredients

| | |
|---|---|
| 2 | cloves garlic, minced |
| 2 | T. light olive oil |
| 1 | T. melted butter |
| 1 | t. dried basil |
| 1/2 | t. salt |
| 1 | t. ground black pepper |
| 3 | T. lemon juice |
| 1 | T. fresh parsley, chopped |
| 2 | (6 oz.) fillets salmon |
| 1 | lemon, cut into 6 to 8 thin slices |

### Chef's Tip

*If your fillets still have the skin, remove it before placing in the marinade. This keeps the fish from smelling too fishy.*

~ 107 ~

# Side Dishes

A side dish, sometimes referred to as a side order or simply a side, is a food item that accompanies the entrée or main course at a meal. A typical meal with a meat-based main dish might include one vegetable side dish, sometimes in the form of a salad, and one starch side dish, such as bread, potatoes, rice, or pasta. Side dishes are considered subordinate to, a main course

A related term is *on the side*. In some instances this is a synonym for side dish, such as "french fries on the side". It can also refer to a sauce, salad dressing, or condiment served in a separate dish from the food item it accompanies. For example, in restaurants one can request that one's side salad be served with dressing on the side.

The name "side dish" could lead one to believe the item in question is of little consequence. Not so. Side dishes, especially within cutting edge restaurants are more than an afterthought. In fact, many chefs consider a "side dish" to be an integral part of the main dish.

In high-end restaurants, side dishes tend to be part of the overall dish, a component of the whole. In most cases, the chef gears the vegetable garnish with a particular dish to complement the protein and the style of cooking, no matter what it is.

Side dishes are as likely to sit among, or even under the entree at high-end restaurants. Standbys, if they exist, are more likely to be unusual, such as roasted garlic custard at Hamersley's Bistro, Boston, or seared polenta cake and fresh spinach with white truffle oil at Pomegranate Euro Bistro, Richmond, Va.

For Your Information: French fries are the most common side dish served at fast-food restaurants and other American cuisine restaurants.

# These dishes stand on their own

*side dish*        Plan - Purchase - Prep - Prepare - Plate - Present

# Awesome Garlic Mash Potatoes

No book on side dishes would be complete without a recipe for mash potatoes. Mash potatoes are one of the ultimate comfort foods of all times. And this one is no exception to that rule.

In this case, we're kicking up the traditional dish by adding two kinds of cheese and fresh chives... not to mention the garlic. By the way, if you're not a big fan of garlic, you can leave that ingredient out, and just make Awesome Mash Potatoes, sans garlic. However, you might want to try this recipe, as described, just once, and you might just decide that garlic is a good thing.

## Plan/Purchase

### Ingredients

| | |
|---|---|
| 1 | lb. Yukon Gold potatoes |
| 1/2 | c. butter |
| 2 | c. Parmesan cheese |
| 1 | c. chopped fresh chives |
| 1 1/2 | c. cream cheese |
| 1/2 | medium head garlic |
| - | salt and pepper, to taste |

### Chef's Tip

*If you're baking an entire garlic head, as the recipe suggests, you will probably not want to use all of the garlic (unless you REALLY love garlic). At the most, half the cloves is all you're going to use. You can always wrap the remaining garlic up in plastic wrap and store in the frig. They will last for two weeks, or more.*

## Prep/Prepare

1. Prepare the garlic, using the method described below.
2. Bring a pot of salted water to a boil. Add potatoes; cook until tender but still firm. Drain and return to stove over low heat to dry for 1 to 2 minutes.
3. Add butter, Parmesan cheese, chives, cream cheese, garlic, salt, and pepper.
4. Use a potato ricer, if you have one, or mash them using a large fork, or potato masher.

## Baked Garlic

5. Place a rack in the middle position, and preheat oven to 350° f.
6. Take a fresh head of garlic, and cut off the point of the taper to expose the cloves.
7. Place on a piece of aluminum foil, drizzle with oil, and then wrap in the foil.
8. Bake in the oven for 20 to 30 minutes.
9. When cool sufficiently, you should be able to pop the garlic cloves out of the head by simply squeezing.

## Plate/Present

If it's a big event, place the potatoes into a large, pre-warmed serving dish, and sprinkle some chopped chives over the top... YUMMY!

If it's more formal, you can place the potatoes on an individual serving plate, along with the other meal items.

*Cooking with a Plan Vol 1: Back to the Kitchen* — side dish

# Pommes Anna

*Pommes Anna (pom-ANNA), is a classic French dish cooked in a very large amount of melted butter. For that reason (even though the butter is eventually discarded), and because the initial preparation is quite meticulous and labor intensive, Pommes Anna is seldom prepared today in its original fashion.*

*This recipe is a combination of great potato taste with a minimum of work. Once you try this dish, you may find yourself serving it more and more. I know that I do.*

## Prep/Prepare

1. Preheat the oven to 400f.
2. Peel and slice the potatoes as thinly as possible.

**Note: Do not put the slices in water, since the starch on the slices is what makes the whole thing stick together.**

3. Liberally brush an 8-inch sauté pan with clarified butter and arrange the potato slices in concentric rings (slices should overlap) emanating from the center of the pan, until you have one layer.
4. Brush the layer with clarified butter and season lightly with salt and pepper.
5. Create more layers, buttering the new layers as you go. Stop when you run out of potatoes, or you fill the pan.

**Note: To make it pretty, you may want to reserve some uniform slices to fan out into a nice design on top.**

6. Place the pan on the stovetop and cook undisturbed over medium heat until golden brown on the bottom, about 3 to 4 minutes.
7. Transfer the potatoes to the oven and cook until caramelized and cooked through, about 30 minutes, pressing the potatoes occasionally to compress, and shaking the pan to keep the potatoes from sticking to the bottom.
8. Bake, until the top is golden brown and crispy (could take up to an hour).

## Plate/Present

Place the potatoes on a serving dish, and then use a large kitchen knife (or pizza wheel), to cut into pie-shape serving pieces.

If you really want to go crazy, sauté some mushrooms in butter and onions, and dress over the top.

## Plan/Purchase

### Ingredients

| | | |
|---|---|---|
| 2 | lb. | large Yukon gold potatoes |
| 1/2 | c. | clarified butter |
| | | Salt and pepper, to taste |

### Pommes Anna Pans

*It you really want to do it up right, you can purchase a Pommes Anna baking set, like the one pictured below. They're typically wrought of heavy copper with a tin lining for safe non-reactive baking, and they'll set you back about two to three hundred bucks.*

*Okay... I'll admit it... I do own a pommes anna pan set. Hey, I'm only human.*

### For Your Information

*In order for the dish to cook evenly, your slices need to be the same thickness. While you could achieve this by using a sharp knife and being very careful not to cut your fingers, the best way is to use a mandoline.*

~ 111 ~

*side dish*  Plan · Purchase · Prep · Prepare · Plate · Present

# Broccoli Casserole

*Broccoli casseroles are not new; as a matter of fact, they've been around for a long, long time. When I was just a lad, my mother always tried to get me to eat things like broccoli; however, it was a waste of time... my sides were corn and potatoes. As I grew up, so did my palette, and my curiosity for different food groups. To my surprise, I discovered that I enjoy a lot of things... including broccoli.*

*If you like broccoli, or you're in an experimental mood, give this side dish a try. I think you'll like it.*

## Plan/Purchase

### Ingredients

| | |
|---|---|
| 2 | c. steamed rice |
| 5 | T. butter |
| 1/2 | c. yellow onion, chopped |
| 20 | oz. steamed broccoli florets |
| 1 | can cream of mushroom soup (like, Campbells) |
| 1 | c. shredded sharp Cheddar cheese |
| 3/4 | c. mayonnaise |
| 2 | eggs, beaten |
| 1/2 | t. garlic, minced |
| 1/4 | t. ground black pepper |
| 2 | t. lemon juice |
| 1 | c. ritz (or other butter cracker), crushed fine |

### Chef's Tip

*I've never been a big fan of using canned soups for anything (I'm a snob); however, in this recipe it works.*

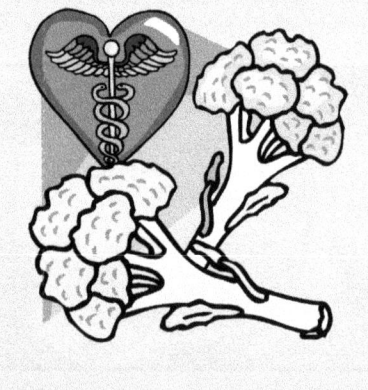

## Prep/Prepare

1. Cook the rice, as directed by the package.
2. Place rack in the bottom position and preheat the oven to 350° f.
3. Melt 3 tablespoons of butter in a small saucepan over medium-high heat, and then saute chopped onions until nice and golden... remove from pan, and set aside.
4. Add 1/2 cup of water to the pan, bring to a boil.
5. Add broccoli florets, cover and steam for about 4 minutes.
6. Mix the rice, onion, broccoli, soup, cheese, mayonnaise, eggs, garlic, pepper, and lemon juice in a baking dish.
7. Dust the top with the crushed crackers and dot with the remaining 2 tablespoons of butter, over the top
8. Bake uncovered in preheated oven for 45 minutes, until heated through and browned on top.

Cooking with a Plan Vol I: Back to the Kitchen        side dish

# Fried Rice with Eggs and Peas

*Fried rice is a popular component of Chinese cuisine, and originated as a home dish around 4000 BC. Traditional fried rice is made from cold leftover rice, fried with other leftover ingredients. Later it became a more elaborate dish, made from fresh ingredients, and often served as the penultimate dish in Chinese banquets (just before dessert).*

*As long as rice is served pure, white and fluffy, all will be well under the heavens (Chinese proverb).*

## Prep/Prepare

1. Cook the rice, and let sit covered in the refrigerator for 24 hours, or up to 3 days.
2. Break up any clumps of the cold rice with your fingers and set aside. See note on rice type, at bottom of this page.
3. In a small bowl, stir together the oyster and soy sauce and set aside.
4. Place skillet over high heat. When hot add the peas and scallions, and cook, stirring constantly, until the scallions are limp, about 1 minute.
5. Stir in the rice, sauce mixture, and eggs until well mixed.
6. Continue to cook, stirring, until the rice is heated through, 1 to 2 minutes. Plate and drizzle with sesame oil, to taste.

## Plate/Present

This is a side dish; however, it can become a main dish quickly. Chicken and/or pork come to mind. If you have an oriental market close by, you might be able to pick up a piece of seasoned, cooked roast pork. Just bring it home, slice it thin, and cook it with the eggs and peas.

This is an oriental staple, so why not begin with warm sake, and sushi rolls.

Serve the meal with chopsticks; however, leave out regular silverware for the timid, or faint of heart.

## What the recipe doesn't know

**What type of rice you're using.** For this recipe, use a good long-grain white rice, cook it 24 hours before using, and store in the refrigerator in a sealed container. This gives the rice a chance to firm up, and prevents it from breaking down in the skillet.

**What's available in your area.** Most grocery stores will have oriental spices and sauces; however, if you have difficulty finding oyster sauce, you can order it on-line at: www.cooks.com, or www.lkk.com.

## Plan/Purchase

### Ingredients

| | |
|---|---|
| 2 | c. long-grain converted white rice, rinsed |
| - | salt, to taste |
| 1/4 | c. oyster sauce |
| 2 | T. light Japanese soy sauce |
| 3 | eggs, beaten until just blended |
| - | peanut or vegetable oil, as needed |
| 1 | c. frozen baby peas, thawed |
| 1/3 | c. scallions, thinly sliced, including some of the green tops |
| 2 | c. diced cooked roast pork, optional |
| | Sesame oil, as needed |

### For Your Information

*Fried rice is a popular component of Asian cuisine. It originated as a home dish from China around 4000 BC. That's what I call a dish with staying power.*

side dish    Plan · Purchase · Prep · Prepare · Plate · Present

# Candied Sweet Potatoes

These are great-tasting sweet potatoes, and don't be drawn off by the "candied" part of the recipe, because these sweet potatoes are not as sweet as most candied recipes.

This recipe is about as simple as you can get, and can be prepared using the same sauce pan.

If you would prefer, you can bake the sweet potatoes by placing them on a parchment-lined baking sheet, and bake in a pre-heated 350° f. oven, for 30 minutes, or until tender.

## Plan/Purchase

### Ingredients

| | |
|---|---|
| 2 | sweet potatoes, large, and cut into cubes |
| 1/4 | c. butter |
| 1/2 | c. packed brown sugar |
| 1/4 | c. fresh squeezed orange juice |
| 12 | mini marshmallows (optional) |

### For Your Information

Sweet potatoes are a large edible root belonging to the morning-glory family

There are many varieties of sweet potato but the two that are widely grown commercially are a pale sweet potato and the darker-skinned variety erroneously call "yam"

## Prep/Prepare

1. Boil cut-up sweet potatoes in a large sauce pan (about 2 quart) until potatoes are tender, but not falling apart, about 20 minutes.
2. Remove sweet potatoes from pan, and set aside.
3. Using the same pan, add butter and brown sugar, and then bring to a simmer. Make sure sugar is completely dissolved.
4. Add orange juice and stir until smooth.
5. Add the sweet potatoes, raise heat slightly, and continue to cook, until potatoes are caramelized, about 20 minutes.

**Note: If syrup is too thin, add a bit more brown sugar.**

## Plate/Present

Place the sweet potatoes into a large serving dish, add a sprinkling of mini marshmallows, if desired, and enjoy.

~ 114 ~

Cooking with a Plan Vol I: Back to the Kitchen     side dish

# Fantasic Green Beans

*Everyone has a recipe for basic green beans. The cool thing about this side dish is that it's easy to make, and goes with just about any main dish; from beef to fish. This is a simple green bean dish without any additions, such as: onions, etc. Hey, it's just some good old green beans.*

*To make sure that your green beans are fresh, before you buy them, pick one up and break it in half... it should give a satisfying snapping sound.*

## Prep/Prepare

1. Add 1/2 cup of water and salt to a saute pan, and then bring to a boil.
2. Add the green beans, and then cover and simmer for 5 to 7 minutes, or until tenter. Remove the green beans from the pan, and set aside. Do not remove the water.
3. Add another 1/2 cup water to the pan, and bring to a simmer.
4. Dissolve the bouillon cube in the simmering water.
5. Return the green beans to the liquid.
6. Add Worcestershire sauce, soy sauce, butter, garlic salt, and pepper to taste.
7. Simmer gently, uncovered, for 15 minutes.

## Plate/Present

Place green beans in a large serving bowl along with the liquid. Use a slotted spoon to serve. You might even throw a piece of Italian parsley... just for decoration.

## Plan/Purchase

### Ingredients

| | |
|---|---|
| 20 | oz. fresh green beans |
| 1/4 | t. salt |
| 1 | cube beef bouillon, like Knorr |
| 1 | T. Worcestershire sauce |
| 1 | t. soy sauce |
| 1 | T. butter |
| 1/8 | t. garlic salt |
| 1/8 | t. pepper |

### For Your Information

*Green beans are long, and slender with small seeds inside. The entire pod is edible.*

*It's also called string bean (because of the fibrous string-now bred out of the species-that used to run down the pod's seam), and snap bean (for the sound the bean makes when broken in half)... SNAP !!!*

~ 115 ~

side dish — Plan · Purchase · Prep · Prepare · Plate · Present

# Baked Beans — Boston style

According to tradition, the dish is was named "Boston" Baked Beans because it was made by Puritan Bostonian women on Saturday, to be served for dinner that night. Since cooking was forbidden on the Sabbath, the leftover beans were served with brown bread for a nice Sunday breakfast.

This recipe is fairly traditional in its approach to making this dish, and requires that the beans be soaked overnight. If you've never tried Boston baked beans, then believe me when I say, the wait is more than worth it.

## Plan/Purchase

### Ingredients

| | |
|---|---|
| 2 | c. navy beans |
| 1/2 | lb. bacon |
| 1 | onion, finely diced |
| 3 | T. molasses |
| 2 | t. salt |
| 1/4 | t. ground black pepper |
| 1/4 | t. dry mustard |
| 1/2 | c. ketchup |
| 1 | T. Worcestershire sauce |
| 1/4 | c. brown sugar |

### Chef's Tip

Halfway through the baking process, stop and take a peek at the beans. Add more of the reserved liquid, if necessary, to prevent the beans from drying out.

## Prep/Prepare

1. Place the beans in a pot of cold water, and leave to soak overnight.
2. Simmer the beans in the same water, until tender, about 1 or 2 hours.
3. Drain and reserve the liquid.
4. Adjust rack to the bottom position of the oven, and then preheat to 325° f.
5. Place a layer of beans in a 2 quart ovenproof pot or casserole dish (about 1 inch thick) and then layer with bacon and onion.
6. Repeat the layering process for the remainder of the ingredients.
7. In a small saucepan over medium high heat, add the molasses, salt, pepper, dry mustard, ketchup, Worcestershire and brown sugar,
8. Allow the mixture to slowly come to the boil, and then, pour over the beans.
9. Add reserved bean water until the beans are covered, but no more.
10. Cover the dish and bake for 3 to 4 hours, until beans are tender.

**Note: Occassionally check the beans, if drying out, add more of the reserved liquid.**

## Plate/Present

This one's easy... place the beans in a big old bowl with a ladle, and let your guests scoop out what they want. I always try to grab a piece of the bacon, before it disappears. It's a great side dish to serve with corn bread, or even some biscuits.

## For Your Information

The current most favored theory on the origin of Boston Baked Beans is that American Indians cooked beans with maple syrup and bear fat. Never wasting fuel, they slow-cooked the beans in coals.

# Spanish Rice

*Traditionally, Spanish rice is a dish made from white rice, tomatoes, garlic, onions, and other ingredients. In addition, the rice is typically toasted, and then cooked in chicken broth. This recipe adds a bit of kick by incorporating some green peppers, and jalapeño chiles. If you or your guests are not fond of heat, you can leave the chilies out.*

*This, by definition, is a side dish; however, on occasion, I find myself making this recipe, serving it with some warm tortillas, and using it as a lite Summer lunch on the patio.*

## Prep/Prepare

1. Add the oil to large saute pan over medium heat, and heat until the oil just begins to shimmer.
2. Add the uncooked rice, onion, jalapeño, garlic, and bell pepper
3. Saute until rice is browned and the onions are translucent, about 10 to 12 minutes.
4. Add the chicken stock and tomatoes, and stir to combine.
5. Season with the chili powder and salt.
6. Cover, and simmer until rice is cooked and liquid is absorbed, about 30 minutes

## Plate/Present

Hey, this is a side dish... put it in a nice serving bowl, add a spoon, and go for it.

### Shopping Tip

It's always best if you can use fresh tomatoes; however, if you don't have access to a farmer's market, and you don't want to buy the tasteless tomatoes, served up at most supermarkets, then you might to try Hunts Petite Diced Tomatoes.

They've won several taste tests, and in my opinion, if I need diced tomatoes, and I can't get fresh, that's probably the brand I'm going to grab.

## Plan/Purchase

### Ingredients

| | |
|---|---|
| 2 | T. olive oil |
| 1 | c. uncooked long grain white rice |
| 1 | onion, chopped |
| 1 | clove garlic, chopped |
| 1/2 | green bell pepper, chopped |
| 2 | c. chicken stock |
| 10 | oz. diced tomatoes |
| 1 | jalapeño chile, seeded & diced |
| 2 | t. chili powder |
| 1 | t. salt |

### Did You Know

*Spanish Rice* was also an album created by Clark Terry and Cuban band leader Chico, O'Farrill. The album was recorded in 1966, and featured Latin tunes.

Hope that helps...

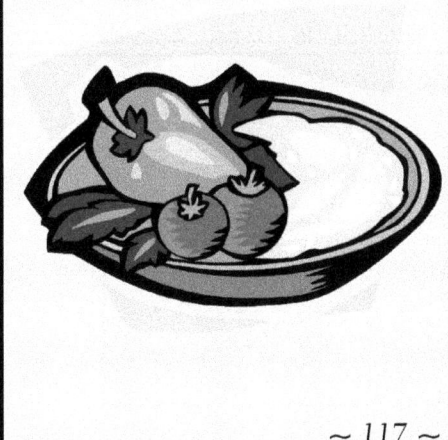

*side dish*       Plan · Purchase · Prep · Prepare · Plate · Present

# Mushroom Risotto

*Making good risotto is like riding a bicycle: It takes a bit of practice; however, once you've got the technique down, you'll never forget.*

*Risotto (rih-SAW-toh). is an Italian rice specialty made by stirring hot stock into a mixture of rice (and often chopped onions) that have been sautéed in butter. This recipe carries on the Italian tradition; along with mushrooms and chives, to kick up the taste.*

## Plan/Purchase

### Ingredients

| | |
|---|---|
| 5 | c. chicken broth |
| 3 | T. olive oil |
| 1 | lb. portobello mushrooms, thinly sliced |
| 1 | lb. white mushrooms, thinly sliced |
| 2 | shallots, diced |
| 1.5 | c. Arborio rice |
| 1.5 | c. dry white wine |
| - | sea salt and black pepper, to taste |
| 3 | T. finely chopped chives |
| 4 | T. butter |
| 1/3 | c. freshly grated Parmesan cheese |

### Chef's Tip

*You can check the rice to see if it's al dente by biting into a kernel. It should resist slightly to the tooth but not be hard in the center.*

### Cooking Tip

*With Risotto it's all about the stirring, you can't leave it, even for a minute. So when starting this dish, make sure you don't have any other pressing matters to attend.*

~ 118 ~

## Prep/Prepare

1. Use a sauce pan to pre-warm the chicken broth.
2. Add 2 tablespoons of olive oil to a large saucepan, using medium-high heat.
3. Stir in mushrooms, and cook until soft, about 3 minutes.
4. Place the contents of the pan in a small bowl, and set aside.
5. Add 1 tablespoon of olive oil to skillet set to medium high, and then add in the shallots
6. Saute for 1 minute, or until fragrant.
7. Add rice, coat with 1 Tablespoon of oil, and stir for about 2 minutes.
8. Pour in the wine, and stir until the wine is fully absorbed.
9. Add 1/2 cup of the warm broth to the rice, and stir until absorbed.
10. Continue to add broth 1/2 cup at a time, stirring, until the liquid is absorbed and the rice is al dente, 15 to 20 minutes.
11. Remove from heat, and stir in mushrooms with their liquid, butter, chives, and Parmesan. Season with salt and pepper to taste.

## Plate/Present

Risotto is a great dish that compliments a lot of main dishes, such as grilled meats, and chicken.

It needs to be served immediately after cooking, or it will become soft. So make sure you use the Plan, and have everything ready, because risotto waits for no one.

Cooking with a Plan Vol 1: Back to the Kitchen    side dish

# Roasted Vegetables

*This is an easy to make side dish, that goes well with just about any dinner. As a matter of fact, you can make the dish the day before, and reheat in the oven, when needed.*

*The vegetables were picked for their flavor, and to add some color to the dish; however, you can add any of your favorite veggies to this dish without problem.*

*As a side dish, roasted vegetables go with just about any main dish, fish or meat, so have some fun, do some experimentation, and enjoy.*

## Prep/Prepare

1. Adjust rack to middle position, and then preheat oven to 475° f.
2. In a large bowl, combine the carrots, red bell peppers, sweet potato, and Yukon Gold potatoes.
3. Separate the red onion quarters into layered pieces, and add to the mixture.
4. Stir in the thyme, rosemary, olive oil, vinegar, salt, and pepper in a separate prep bowl.
5. Toss the vegetables with the mixture until well coated.
6. Spread the vegetables on a large baking sheet lined with parchment paper.
7. Roast for 35 to 40 minutes, or until the veggies are cooked through and nicely browned.

**Note: Stir once or twice during the baking.**

## Plate/Present

To keep them nice and warm, serve them in a pre-heated, covered dish.

## Plan/Purchase

### Ingredients

| | |
|---|---|
| 2 | medium carrots, cubed |
| 1 | red bell pepper, seeded and diced |
| 1/2 | medium sweet potato, peeled and cubed |
| 2 | Yukon Gold potatoes, cubed |
| 1/2 | red onion, quartered |
| 1 | t. chopped fresh thyme |
| 2 | t. chopped fresh rosemary |
| 1.5 | T. olive oil |
| 2 | t. balsamic vinegar |
| | salt and ground black pepper, to taste |

# Sweets

Having an agreeable taste or flavor such as that of sugar; saccharine; -- opposed to sour and bitter; as, a sweet beverage; sweet fruits; sweet oranges.

Pleasing to the smell; fragrant; redolent; balmy; as, a sweet rose; sweet odor; sweet incense. The term sweet is sometimes referred to as a confectionery.

Confectionery refers to food items that are (or perceived to be) rich in sugar.

In Britain, Ireland and some Commonwealth countries, "sweets", or "sweeties", particularly in Scotland (sweeties resembles the Scottish Gaelic word suiteis in both pronunciation and meaning) and among children. In some parts of England, spice and goodies are terms used, alongside sweets, to denote confectionery.

In Australia and New Zealand, they are referred to as "lollies", and in North America, "candy" -

The term "sweet" can also refer to a specific range of confectionery and does not include some items called confectionery (e.g. pastry).

Confectionery items include sweets, lollipops, candy bars, chocolate, and other sweet items of snack food. The term does not generally apply to cakes, biscuits, or puddings which require cutlery to consume, although exceptions such as petits fours or meringues exist.

American English classifies many confections as candy. Some of the categories and types of candy include:

Hard candy: Based on sugars cooked to the hard-crack stage, including suckers (known as boiled sweets in British English), lollipops, jawbreakers (or gobstoppers), lemon drops, peppermint drops and disks, candy canes, rock candy, etc.

Fudge: A confection of milk and sugar boiled to the soft-ball stage. In the US, it tends to be chocolate-flavored.

Toffee (or Taffy): Based on sugars cooked to the soft-ball stage and then pulled to create an elastic texture. In British English, toffee refers to a harder substance also made from cooked sugars.

# for the sweet

Swiss Milk Tablet. A crumbly milk-based soft candy, based on sugars cooked to the soft-ball stage. Comes in several forms, such as wafers and heart shapes.

Licorice: Containing extract of the liquorice root. Chewier and more resilient than gum/gelatin candies, but still designed for swallowing.

Chocolates: Used in the plural, usually referring to small balled centers covered with chocolate to create bite-sized confectionery. People who create chocolates are called chocolatiers, and they create their confections with couverture chocolate. A chocolate maker, on the other hand, is the person who physically creates the couverture from cacao beans and other ingredients.

Kopiko: A coffee flavored sweet made in Asia.

Gum/Gelatin candies: Based on gelatins, including gum drops, jujubes, Lokum / Turkish Delight, jelly beans, gummies, etc.

Marshmallow: "Peeps" (a trade name), circus peanuts, etc.

Marzipan: An almond-based confection, doughy in consistency, served in several different ways. It is often formed into shapes mimicking (for example) fruits or animals. Alternatively, marzipan may be flavored, normally with spirits such as Kirsch or Rum, and divided into small bite-sized pieces; these flavored marzipans are generally served coated in chocolate to prevent the alcohol from evaporating, and are very common in northern Europe. Marzipan is also used in cake decoration. Its lower-priced version is called Persipan.

Divinity: A nougat-like confectionery based on egg whites with chopped nuts.

And so, that's probably about everything that you every wanted to know about sweets, and a whole bunch more, so let's get cooking.

sweets — Plan · Purchase · Prep · Prepare · Plate · Present

# Scottish Shortbread

In the 1750's Scottish shortbread was a festival bread. It was made around Christmas, and like all old recipes, varied and changed between those making it. The traditional proportion of ingredients for a shortbread are 1 part sugar, 2 parts butter, and 3 parts flour.

I love Scottish shortbread, in fact I used to buy it all the time... that is until I found out how easy it was to make. Believe me, there is nothing like the smell and taste of freshly baked shortbread.

## Plan/Purchase

### Ingredients

- 2 c. butter
- 1 c. packed brown sugar
- 4 1/2 c. all-purpose flour

### Chef's Tip

Although not traditional, adding 2 teaspoons of vanilla and 1/2 teaspoon of salt really adds great flavor.

### Variation

Although the recipe calls for the use of white flour (the traditional flour for shortbread cookies), there's nothing to prevent you from trying out other flours such as: whole wheat, or even spelt.

## Prep/Prepare

1. Preheat oven to 325° f.
2. Cream butter and brown sugar, and then add 3 to 3 3/4 cups flour. Mix well.
3. Sprinkle board with the remaining flour. Knead for 5 minutes, adding enough flour to make a soft dough.
4. Roll to 1/2-inch thickness. Cut into 3x1 inch rectangular strips. Prick with fork and place on ungreased baking sheets.
5. Bake at 325° f. for 20 to 25 minutes.

## Plate/Present

These are cookies, so don't worry about how to plate or present them; however, with that said, I do like these with a nice cup of coffee, or a steaming pot of tea.

## For Your Information

Scotland is credited as the birthplace of shortbread.

Scottish bakers fought to prevent shortbread from being classified as a biscuit to avoid paying a government tax on biscuits.

In Scotland you can find regional variations. For example, in Shetland and Orkney the people add caraway seeds and call it "Bride's Bonn." At holiday time in Edinburgh, shortbread is commonly adorned with pieces of citrus peel and almonds.

Shortbread has a reputation as being a tea-time accompaniment, but it is also enjoyed with milk, coffee, wine, or even a flute of champagne.

# Coconut Macaroons with chocolate centers

*[mak-uh-ROON] A small cookie classically made of almond paste or ground almonds (or both) mixed with sugar and egg whites. Almond macaroons can be chewy, crunchy or a combined texture with the outside crisp and the inside chewy.*

*In this recipe you will substitute coconut for the almonds, and add a bit of flavor by creating a chocolate center. As treats go, these are great tasting, and if you serve them to your guests, make sure that you have enough.*

## Prep/Prepare

**Cookies**

1. Preheat oven to 350.
2. Combine egg whites, sugar and coconut in a bowl.
3. Press tablespoons of the mixture onto a parchment-lined cookie sheet, to make thin circles, about 2 inches.
4. Bake 15 minutes, until golden brown.

**Prepare Filling**

5. Place the cream in a saucepan, and bring almost to a boil.
6. Remove from heat and stir in the chocolate, butter, and orange zest until smooth.
7. Let cool slightly, until beginning to thicken.
8. Take one of the macaroons and cover generously with the filling.
9. Place another cookie on top (like a sandwich).
10. Repeat for remaining cookies, and then refrigerate for several hours.

## Plate/Present

*Hey, these are cookies... just put them on a plate and then stand back.*

*If you're a traditionalist, serve them with a glass of cold milk. If you're not, serve them with anything that you like; even a glass of white wine.*

*If it's Christmas time, you might want to leave some out for Santa. Actually, that's a sure-fire way to get the big guy to come visit your house, and just might guarantee some really cool presents.*

## Plan/Purchase

### Cookie

| | |
|---|---|
| 3 | egg whites |
| 3/4 | cup sugar |
| 3 | c. coconut |

### Filling

| | |
|---|---|
| 1/4 | cup cream |
| 3 | oz dark chocolate |
| 1 | oz butter |
| | zest from 1 orange |

### Did You Know

*According to legend, the macaroon was invented in an Italian monastery in 1792.*

*Later, two Carmelite nuns, hiding in the town of Nancy during the French Revolution, baked and sold macaroons to cover their expenses.*

*They became known as the "Macaroon Sisters."*

sweets                    Plan · Purchase · Prep · Prepare · Plate · Present

# Classic Apple Pie

*Samuel Sewall, (1696) of Harvard College, went on a picnic expedition to Hog Island on October 1, 1697. There he dined on a dinner with a conclusion of apple pie. That is the first historical mention of apple pie in American history... Isn't that exciting.*

*No cookbook would be complete without a recipe for good ole' American apple pie. Here's a classic recipe that has tart apple flavor in every bite. Serve it warm, with a scoop of vanilla ice cream and you have one fantastic dessert.*

## Plan/Purchase

### Dough

| | |
|---|---|
| 2 1/2 | c. all-purpose flour |
| 1/4 | c. sugar |
| 1/2 | t. table salt |
| 8 | oz. unsalted butter, cubed |
| 1/4 | c. ice water |

### Filling

| | |
|---|---|
| 4 | **Granny Smith apples, peeled, cored, sliced 1/2" thick** |
| 4 | **Braeburn apples, peeled, cored, sliced 1/2" thick** |
| 1 | c. sugar |
| 1/2 | c. all-purpose flour |
| 1 | T. dark rum, optional |
| 1 | t. ground cinnamon |
| 1/2 | t. kosher salt |
| | **Pinch ground nutmeg** |

## Prep/Prepare

1. Combine flour, sugar, and salt for the dough in a large bowl.
2. Blend in butter with a pastry blender or two knives until pea-size.
3. Stir in water until dough adheres to itself but isn't sticky. Cut the dough in half, and wrap the halves in plastic, and chill 30 minutes.
4. Preheat oven to 450° with rack in the lower third.
5. Toss filling ingredients together in a large bowl and set aside.
6. Roll out the first dough disk on a floured surface to about 12" across and 1/4" thick; transfer to a 9" glass pie plate. Fill with apple filling, drizzling any juices over the fruit. Roll out the other dough disk to about 14" across. Transfer to the pie, crimp edges, and cut steam vents on top.
7. Brush top with half and half, then sprinkle with sugar. Place pie on a baking sheet and bake in the lower portion of the oven for 25 minutes. Reduce temperature to 350° and bake until crust is brown on the bottom and juices are bubbly and thick, about 40 more minutes. Cool completely on a rack before serving.

*Cooking with a Plan Vol 1: Back to the Kitchen*  sweets

# Deep Dish Brownies

*In American cooking, a chocolate brownie, also known as a brownie or a Boston brownie, is a small, rich, chocolate, baked cake-slice, named after its brown color. The first known mention of a brownie is believed to be in the 1897 Sears catalog.*

*Folklore reports that the brownie was invented at the Palmer House Hotel in Chicago during the 1892 Columbian Exposition. Bertha Palmer requested a dessert to put in box lunches for ladies that would not get their hands dirty.*

## Prep/Prepare

1. Adjust rack to middle position in oven, and then preheat to 350° f.
2. Put some oil on a paper towel, and then wipe the inside of an 8 inch square baking pan.
3. Blend the butter, sugar and vanilla in a bowl.
4. Whip in the eggs one at a time.
5. Combine the flour, cocoa, and salt in a separate bowl, and then blend into the egg mixture.
6. Spread the batter into the prepared pan.
7. Bake 40 to 45 minutes. Brownies should begin to pull away from the sides of the pan.
8. Let cool for 30 minutes on a wire rack.

## Plate/Present

*I think that I would let them cool, then cut them into squares. Then I would take a nice white plate, and pile them on like a small pyramid.*

## Plan/Purchase

### Ingredients

| | |
|---|---|
| 3/4 | c. butter, melted |
| 1 1/2 | c. white sugar |
| 1 1/2 | t. vanilla extract |
| 2 | eggs |
| 3/4 | c. all-purpose flour |
| 1/2 | c. unsweetened cocoa powder |
| 1/2 | t. salt |

### Tasty Additions

Nuts of almost any kind are acceptable.

How about covering them with a nice gooey fudge sauce.

### Chef's Tip

These brownies are simple, unadorned, easy to make, and taste awesome.

~ 125 ~

Plan - Purchase - Prep - Prepare - Plate - Present

# Carrot Cake with cream cheese frosting

When I first heard about carrot cake, I had the impression of something that would impress Bugs Bunny... lots of carrots. Boy, was I wrong. Yes carrot cake, strangely enough, does contain carrots; however, the blending of carrots with the other ingredients, and then topping the whole thing off with a fantastic cream cheese frosting, makes this one of my favorite sweet-tooth treats. Try it, and see if you don't agree.

## Plan/Purchase

### Ingredients

| | |
|---|---|
| 3 | c. unbleached flour |
| 2 | c. granulated sugar |
| 1 | t. salt |
| 1 | T. baking soda |
| 1 | T. ground cinnamon |
| 1.5 | c. corn oil |
| 4 | eggs, lightly beaten |
| 1 | T. vanilla extract |
| 1.5 | c. shelled walnuts, chopped |
| 1.5 | c. shredded coconut |
| 1.3 | c. pureed cooked carrots |
| 3/4 | c. drained crushed pineapple |
| - | cream-cheese frosting of your choice |
| - | confectioners' sugar, for dusting top |

## Prep/Prepare

1. Preheat oven to 350° f., grease two 9-in layer cake pans, and line with parchment paper
2. Sift dry ingredients into bowl, and then add oil, eggs and vanilla. Beat well.
3. Fold in walnuts, coconut, carrots, and pineapple.
4. Pour batter into pans.
5. Bake on middle rack for 30 to 35 minutes, until edges pull away from sides, and a toothpick inserted into the middle comes out clean.
6. Cool for three hours.
7. Lay one of the cake layers on a platter, and cover the top with cream cheese frosting.
8. Lay the second cake layer on top, and then frost top and sides with cream cheese frosting.
9. Sprinkle some confectioners' sugar over the top.

## Ingredient Tip

There are a lot of good cream cheese frostings on the market, or you could make your own using fresh cream cheese, and sugar.

Cooking with a Plan Vol I: Back to the Kitchen

# Mango Coconut Parfait with honey and yogurt

*A traditional parfait consists of ice cream layered with flavored syrup or fruit and whipped cream, and it can be topped with whipped cream, nuts and even a maraschino cherry.*

*This recipe provides a tasty twist to the traditional parfait, and don't let the lack of ingredients fool you, this baby is packed with sweet flavor, and balances that sweetness with a bit of tart. It's great at the end of a Summer party, or just about any time, you want a great dessert.*

## Prep/Prepare

1. In a small bowl, combine the yogurt and maple syrup, and then keep refrigerated until ready to use.
2. Divide 3/4 cup mango cubes between 4 parfait glasses.
3. Add three or four raspberries.
4. Top each with 2 tablespoons of coconut.
5. Place 1/2 cup yogurt/maple syrup sauce in each glass. Shake the glass slightly to allow some of the yogurt to distribute between the mango cubes.
6. Divide the remaining 3/4 cup mango between each glass.
7. Add a few raspberries over the top, and then sprinkle with 2 tablespoons of coconut.
8. Place a sprig of mint on top, for a garnish.

## Plate/Present

This dish looks its best when served in clear-glass containers. That way your audience can see (and appreciate) the nice colors and contrasts. For example, when you put the raspberries on the first layer (step 3), make sure that they're positioned on the edges of the glass. That way, your guests can see them.

Does doing this make the dish taste better? Well, there's an old chef's expression: We eat first with our eyes.

## Plan/Purchase

### Ingredients

| | |
|---|---|
| 2 | c. plain yogurt, (you can use lowfat, nonfat or whole milk yogurt) |
| 3 | T. pure maple syrup |
| 1 | ripe medium mango, peeled, pitted, and cut into 1/2-inch cubes (1 1/2 cups) |
| 1 | c. sweetened coconut, lightly toasted |
| 1 | small box raspberries |
| - | fresh mint leaves |

### Shopping Tip

*Fresh mango is definitely a mid-to-late Summer fruit. However, this is a dessert that I don't like to reserve just for warm Summer evenings.*

*Although I'll always opt for fresh, I've found several varieties of frozen, cubed mango, that are acceptable (always look for organic).*

~ 127 ~

*sweets*  Plan · Purchase · Prep · Prepare · Plate · Present

# Pecan Coffee Cake

*A cake served with coffee or eaten at breakfast. Under this definition, a coffee cake does not necessarily contain coffee. Coffee cakes are typically flavored with cinnamon, nuts, and fruits. Apples are also a common fruit to add as an ingredient to this dessert.*

*This recipe creates a coffee cake without all the bother, and it tastes great to boot. Serve it at breakfast with coffee (hence the name), or with any beverage, at any time of the day.*

## Plan/Purchase

### Ingredients

| | |
|---|---|
| 2 | c. all-purpose flour |
| 1/4 | t. salt |
| 1 | T. baking powder |
| 1 | c. butter, softened |
| 1 | c. sour cream |
| 1.5 | c. white sugar |
| 2 | eggs |
| 1 | T. vanilla extract |
| 1/2 | c. brown sugar |
| 1 | c. chopped pecans |
| 1 | t. ground cinnamon |
| 2 | T. butter, melted |

### Chef's Tip

Don't forget that oven temperature is critical to any baking job. You should pre-heat the oven for about twenty minutes, to help stabilize the cooking temperature.

In addition, it's not a bad idea to have your ovens calibrated once and awhile.

Baking is all about the ingredients; however, it's also about accurate temperature.

## Prep/Prepare

1. Preheat oven to 350° f.
2. Line a 9x13 inch pan with aluminum foil or parchment paper, and lightly grease with vegetable oil or cooking spray.
3. Sift together the flour, baking powder, and salt; set aside.
4. In a large bowl, cream the butter until light and fluffy. Gradually beat in sour cream, then beat in sugar. Beat in the eggs one at a time, then stir in the vanilla.
5. By hand, fold in the flour mixture, mixing just until incorporated.
6. Spread batter into prepared pan.
7. To make the Pecan Topping: In a medium bowl, mix together brown sugar, pecans and cinnamon. Stir in melted butter until crumbly. Sprinkle over cake batter in pan.
8. Bake in the preheated oven for 30 to 35 minutes, or until a toothpick inserted into the center of the cake comes out clean. Let cool in pan for 10 minutes, then turn out onto a wire rack.

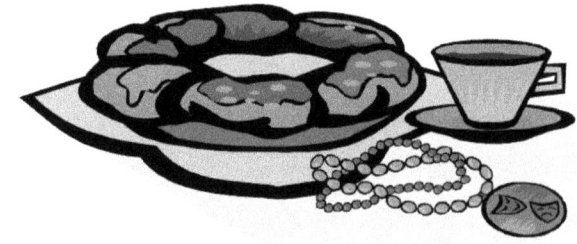

# Pecan Lace Cookies

*These cookies are light and lacy, and are brimming with sweet pecan flavor. These confections are between a cookie and a candy. The caramelized brown sugar flavor is reminiscent of Pecan Pralines from New Orleans, but are delicate and lacy.*

*In the oven, they spread into perfectly flat rounds that can be molded, while warm, into cups, cones, or cigarettes. While the ingredients are simple, and the baking process is straightforward, that doesn't mean that your guests won't be impressed.*

## Prep/Prepare

1. Preheat oven to 350°f, and position rack in center of oven
2. Line 2 baking sheets with parchment paper
3. Stir butter, sugar, and corn syrup in saucepan over low heat until melted and smooth
4. Bring to boil over medium-high heat, stirring constantly
5. Remove from heat
6. Stir in flour, and then stir in nuts and vanilla
7. Drop dough by teaspoonfuls onto baking sheet (2 inches apart)
8. Bake until bubbly and lightly browned (about 11 minutes)
9. Cool completely before removing from sheet

## Plate/Present

Presentation here is simple, just let them cool, place them on a nice plate. You might even want to dust them with a bit of confectionery sugar.

Just remember to get out of the way of your hungry guests, as they grab a handful of these tasty delights.

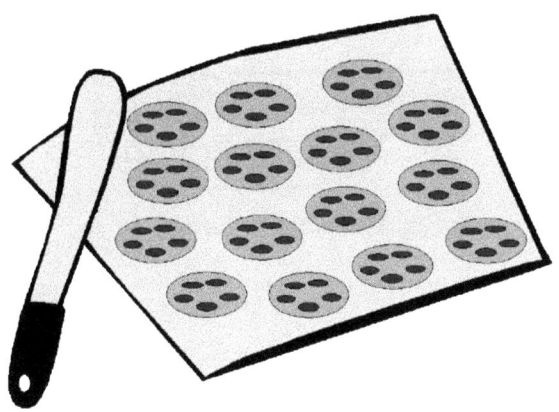

## Plan/Purchase

### Ingredients

| | |
|---|---|
| 1/4 | c. unsalted butter, at room temperature |
| 1/3 | c. sugar |
| 2 | T. light corn syrup |
| 1/3 | c. all-purpose flour |
| 1 | c. coarsely ground pecans (4 oz) |
| 1 | t. vanilla extract |

### Chef's Tip

*Lace cookies are very thin and delicate, so let them cool a bit before removing them from the baking sheet.*

*This also gives you the opportunity to experiment with the cookies. For example, while they are still a bit warm, you could try bending them into other shapes; like a cone or curve.*

*In other words, why do cookies have to be flat.*

sweets                    Plan - Purchase - Prep - Prepare - Plate - Present

# Pecan Pralines

*I got hooked on praline candies when I was doing my undergraduate work at Tennessee. I've always wanted to repeat that experience, so I came up with this recipe. It's a simple recipe to make, and it's packed with Southern tradition and flavor. Give them a try on some quite Summer night.*

*I hope they remind you of lightning bugs, mint juleps on the veranda, and warm blessed evenings in the South. Can't you just feel that breeze flowing though the Magnolias?*

## Plan/Purchase

### Ingredients

| | |
|---|---|
| 1.5 | c. toasted pecans |
| 1.5 | c. white sugar |
| 3/8 | c. butter |
| 3/4 | c. brown sugar |
| 1/2 | c. milk |
| 1 | t. vanilla extract |

### Chef's Tip

You'll want to watch the candies as they cook... if they go too long they will have a bitter flavor.

Therefore, use the cooking times in a general sense, and remove them when they pass the soft-ball test.

## Prep/Prepare

1. Line a baking sheet with parchment paper.
2. In a large saucepan over medium heat, combine pecans, sugar, butter, brown sugar, milk and vanilla.
3. Heat to 240° f. or until a small amount of syrup dropped into cold water forms a soft ball that flattens when removed from the water and placed on a flat surface.
4. Drop by spoonfuls onto prepared baking sheet.
5. Let cool completely... no baking required.

### Equipment Tip

If you do a lot of candy making, you might want to invest in a candy thermometer. That way, if the liquid needs to be an exact temperature, you'll know to the degree.

# Apple Crisp

*Crunchy apples especially from Washington state are the inspiration for many baked apple dishes, and this one is no exception.*

*Apple crisp in the United States or Apple crumble as it is known in the United Kingdom is a dessert consisting of baked apples topped with a crispy crust. Ingredients usually include cooked apples, butter, sugar, flour, cinnamon, and often oats and brown sugar, ginger, and/or nutmeg. Oh, and don't forget the vanilla ice cream.*

## Prep/Prepare

1. Preheat oven to 350° f.
2. Place the sliced apples in a 9x13 inch pan. Mix the white sugar, 1 tablespoon flour and ground cinnamon together, and sprinkle over apples. Pour water evenly over all.
3. Combine the oats, 1 cup flour, brown sugar, baking powder, baking soda and melted butter together. Crumble evenly over the apple mixture.
4. Bake in preheated oven for about 45 minutes.

## Plate/Present

*Apple crisp is best served warm... on a nice plate with a scoop of homemade vanilla ice cream, and a cherry on top.*

## Plan/Purchase

### Ingredients

| | |
|---|---|
| 10 | c. thinly sliced apples |
| 1 | c. white sugar |
| 1 | T. all-purpose flour |
| 1 | t. ground cinnamon |
| 1/2 | c. water |
| 1 | c. quick-cooking oats |
| 1 | c. all-purpose flour |
| 1 | c. packed brown sugar |
| 1/4 | t. baking powder |
| 1/4 | t. baking soda |
| 1/2 | c. butter, melted |

### Did You Know

*The earliest reference to apple crisp in print occurred in 1924, in the Everybody's Cook Book: A Comprehensive Manual of Home Cookery.*

*In the same year, it also made an appearance in a newspaper article in the Appleton Post Crescent on Tuesday, December 09, 1924 (Appleton, Wisconsin).*

# Soup

A liquid food prepared from meat, fish, or vegetable stock combined with various other ingredients and often containing solid pieces.

Theoretically, a soup can be any combination of vegetables, meat or fish cooked in a liquid. It may be thick (like gumbo), thin (such as a consommé), smooth (like a bisque) or chunky (chowder or bouillabaisse). Though most soups are hot, some like vichyssoise and many fruit soups are served cold. Soups are often garnished with flavor enhancers such as croutons, grated or cubed cheese or sour cream. They can be served as a first course or as a meal, in which case they're often accompanied by a sandwich or salad.

A soup may be the first of several courses, intended just to whet the appetite; it may be one of many dishes served at the same time; or it may be a hearty meal in a bowl. The bottom line is that in order to be a soup, it must be enough of a liquid preparation that eventually one gets around to sipping it, or eating it with a spoon.

Soup is an important mainstay in the everyday diet of most cultures. It was probably one of the earliest cooked preparations because it could be made with just about anything (including leftovers from the day before) and could be extended greatly by adding more liquid. Where food is scarce, soup is a staple: The moral of the "Stone Soup" fable is that soup can be made from nothing at all but stones, water, and generosity.

Although classic French cuisine developed as a result of the availability of many types of food and involves many courses, it has also given soup a place of singular importance. According to the eighteenth-century French gastronome Grimod de la Reynière (1758–1838), "It [soup] is to dinner what a portico or a peristyle is to a building; that is to say, it is not only the first part of it, but it must be devised in such a manner as to set the tone of the whole banquet, in the same way as the overture of an opera announces the subject of the work." In other words, soup should inspire, set the stage, for the rest of the meal.

As the commercial says: Soup is Good Food.

# for the soul

soup

Plan · Purchase · Prep · Prepare · Plate · Present

# Hearty Beef Chili with kidney beans

Chili is one of those dishes that can start a bar fight. What I mean is that most good cooks have their own way to make chili, and most consider their recipe the best of the best. For example, some claim that authentic chile does not have any beans, and others maintain that it does.

In my opinion, the place that best forms a true definition of chili is the great State of Texas. Those folks know their chili. So, not wanting to offend anyone, or to start any bar fights, here's my idea of a great bowl of chili.

## Plan/Purchase

### Ingredients

| | |
|---|---|
| 2 | T. vegetable oil or corn oil |
| 2 | medium onions chopped fine |
| 1 | red bell pepper cut into 1/2-inch cubes |
| 6 | medium cloves of garlic, minced (about 2 T.) |
| 1/4 | c. chili powder |
| 1 | T. ground cumin |
| 2 | t. ground coriander |
| 1 | t. red pepper flakes |
| 1 | t. dried oregano |
| 1/2 | t. cayenne pepper |
| 2 | lb. sirloin, cut into chunks |
| 2 | 16 oz. cans dark red kidney beans, drained and rinsed |
| 1 | 28 oz. can diced tomatoes with juice |
| 1 | 28 oz. can tomato puree |
| | table salt |

## Prep/Prepare

1. Heat oil in large heavy-bottomed Dutch oven over medium heat until shimmering but not smoking, 3 to 4 minutes.
2. Sear sirloin in small batches until browned on all sides. Remove from pot and set aside.
3. Add onions, bell pepper, garlic, chili powder, cumin, coriander, pepper flakes, oregano, and cayenne; cook, stirring occasionally, about five minutes.
4. Return the sirloin to the pan, and continue cooking until vegetables are softened and starting to brown, about five additional minutes.
5. Add beans, tomatoes, tomato puree, and 1/2 teaspoon salt; bring to boil, then reduce heat to low and simmer, covered, stirring occasionally, for 1 hour.
6. Remove cover and continue to simmer 1 hour longer, stirring occasionally until beef is tender and chili is dark, rich, and slightly thickened.
7. Adjust seasoning with additional salt, if necessary.

## Chef's Tip

If the chili begins to overly thicken (and it probably will), no big deal. Simply stir in some water, and continue to simmer.

~ 134 ~

Cooking with a Plan Vol I: Back to the Kitchen — SOUP

# Hamburger Vegetable Soup with barley

*This a simple soup to prepare; however, don't let its simple ingredients fool you. The hamburger and vegetables combine to create deep flavor, and the barley imparts a creamy texture to this great-tasting soup.*

*Soup has always been one of those essential comfort foods for me, and always a welcome addition on those cold Winter evenings, when the snow is blowing, and the wind is howling... that is, unless you live in Hawaii. Even so, soup spells comfort.*

## Prep/Prepare

1. Brown the beef in a heavy-bottom pot or dutch oven.
2. Remove from pot and drain thoroughly.
3. Return beef to pot, and add remaining ingredients.
4. Bring to a boil, and then reduce to a slow simmer.
5. Simmer for one hour, covered, until vegetables are tender, and the browth is smooth and silky.

## For Your Information

*Vegetable Soup was an educational children's television program produced by the New York State Education Department that originally ran for 78 episodes from 1975 to 1978. The show featured the voices of Bette Midler, James Earl Jones (Starwars), and Daniel Stern (City Slickers). WOW!*

## Plan/Purchase

### Ingredients

| | |
|---|---|
| 1.5 | lb. hamburger |
| 6 | c. water |
| 3 | beef cubes (like Knorr) |
| 2 | c. sliced carrots |
| 1.5 | c. coarsely chopped onions |
| 1.5 | c. chopped celery |
| 1/2 | c. chopped green pepper |
| 1/3 | c. barley |
| 1 | t. salt |
| 1 | t. pepper |
| 2 | bay leaves |
| 28 | oz. canned tomatoes chopped w/juice |
| 8 | oz. tomato sauce |

~ 135 ~

# Poached Garlic Soup with thyme & pepper cream

When I saw how much garlic is used in this recipe, I was a bit skeptical; however, over the years it has become one of my favorite recipes for a Fall season soup. It is robust and rich and certainly keeps any vampires at bay. The call for 12 heads, not cloves, of garlic is correct; however, don't worry, poaching the garlic in chicken stock will concentrate and mellow the flavor, and the heavy cream will pull all the tastes together. This recipe makes approximately 6 servings.

This soup goes great with the thyme and red pepper cream recipe, in the sauce section.

## Plan/Purchase

### Ingredients

| | |
|---|---|
| 6 | c. sodium-free vegetable or chicken stock |
| 12 | medium heads of garlic, cloves pulled apart from the root, but not peeled |
| 1 | T. kosher salt |
| 1 | t. freshly-ground pepper |
| 1 | 1/2 c. heavy cream |
| 2 | T. freshly squeezed lemon juice |

### Tip

*Soup cools fairly fast... pre-warming the bowls or mugs in a warm oven (135°f), will keep the soup at the perfect serving temperature.*

## Prep/Prepare

1. Combine the chicken stock, garlic, and salt in a large saucepan and bring to a boil. Reduce the heat and slow simmer, uncovered, until the garlic is very soft (about 1 hour).

**Note:** Since most stocks contain a lot of salt, if your stock is not low or sodium free, DO NOT add the salt.

2. Strain the contents of the pan through a fine sieve. Reserve the chicken stock and garlic in separate bowls.
3. Pop the garlic cloves out of their skins and push the pulp through a sieve.
4. Add the garlic purée into the reserved chicken stock and whisk until combined.
5. Add the pepper, cream and lemon juice, and whisk to combine.
6. Warm the soup over medium-low heat, stirring frequently.

**Note:** You can cool the soup, then keep it covered in the refrigerator for up to 1 day. Reheat before serving.

## Plate/Present

With this soup, a little goes a long way, so it should be prepared with other dishes. For example, you could serve a small bowl of garlic soup along with a side salad, on a cold Fall afternoon... I'm loving it already.

Or it could be used as a starter before the evening meal. Plate the soup using small white bowls, or, small white mugs. The white of the mugs compliments the color of the soup and the red-pepper cream (if used).

Not only do the thyme and pepper creams (recipe in the sauce section) present a visual color contrast, they also give the soup a bit of kick.

Place the soup into small bowls or mugs and, if using the sauce, drizzle a spoonful of each of the creams over the top. Create alternating swirling patterns with each of the creams... Be creative.

# Clam Chowder with pancetta

*Classic clam chowder is a great soup... if you can find some that doesn't taste like it came from a can, that's been sitting on the grocery shelf.*

*Fresh clams are always the best way to go; however, they're not always in season, and being land-locked in Kansas (my home), sometimes makes that a bit difficult. The remedy is to find yourself a good fish monger, and find out when they're getting a shipment of fresh clams. Although there are some canned varieties of clams, fresh is the best way.*

## Prep/Prepare

1. In a Dutch oven over medium heat, sauté the pancetta until crisp, about 5 minutes.
2. Pour off all but 1 Tbs. of the fat, then melt the butter in the pan.
3. Add the onion, celery, garlic and thyme and cook, stirring occasionally, until the onion is soft, 3 to 5 minutes.
4. Add the flour and cook for 1 minute more. Add the potatoes, bay leaves and clam juice-water mixture and bring to a boil.
5. Reduce the heat and simmer until the potatoes are tender, about 15 minutes.
6. Stir in the cream, Worcestershire, salt, black pepper and cayenne.
7. Using a fork, lightly mash the potatoes against the side of the pot to thicken the soup.
8. Add the clams and cook for 2 minutes. Remove the bay leaves and discard.
9. Ladle the soup into warmed bowls and garnish with the chives. Serves 8.

## Chef's Tip

**Shucking Clams**: Working with 1 clam at a time, hold it over a bowl to catch the juices. Place the blade of a clam knife horizontally across the shell and squeeze to open. Using the tip of the knife, remove the clam meat by cutting it away from the shell; place the meat in a separate bowl. Strain the juices through a fine-mesh sieve lined with cheesecloth into a bowl. Add enough water to the juices to total 5 cups. Coarsely chop the clam meat. Set aside.

## Plan/Purchase

### Ingredients

| | |
|---|---|
| 6 | **lb. littleneck clams, rinsed well** |
| 6 | **oz. pancetta, diced** |
| 3 | **T. unsalted butter** |
| 1 | **yellow onion, diced** |
| 2 | **celery stalks, diced** |
| 2 | **garlic cloves, minced** |
| 2 | **t. chopped fresh thyme** |
| 2 | **T. all-purpose flour** |
| 2 | **lb. Yukon Gold potatoes, peeled and diced** |
| 2 | **bay leaves** |
| 1 | **c. heavy cream** |
| 2 | **t. Worcestershire sauce** |
| - | **Salt and freshly ground black pepper, to taste** |
| - | **Pinch of cayenne pepper** |
| 1 | **T. chopped fresh chives (optional).** |

# Potato Soup Supreme

*This soup is outrageous... not only does it have the classic ingredient (potatoes); but it's got all kinds of other goodies, like ham and cheddar cheese. This is a great soup for those cold Winter's nights, as you sit by the fire, and watch the snow falling.*

*But don't wait for Fall or Old Man Winter to come knocking at your door. Serve this soup in the early Spring, or late Summer, when the days begin to turn a bit cooler.*

## Plan/Purchase

### Ingredients

| | |
|---|---|
| 2 | T. olive oil |
| 3 | c. peeled and cubed golden potatoes |
| 1/2 | c. celery, chopped |
| 1/2 | c. onion, chopped |
| 1 | cube chicken bouillon |
| 1 | c. water |
| 1 | t. dried parsley |
| 1/2 | t. salt |
| 1/4 | t. ground black pepper |
| 2 | t. all-purpose flour |
| 1 1/2 | c. milk |
| 1 1/2 | c. cheddar cheese, shredded |
| 1 | c. chopped ham |

### Chef's Tip

*The thickness of this soup, depends on the absorption of liquids by the potatoes, the cooking time, and the exact heat of the pot.*

*I find that the soup usually needs a bit more liquid, so keep some milk or water on hand, and add a bit as the cooking progresses.*

## Prep/Prepare

1. Add olive oil to a large pot over medium high heat, and saute the celery and onions.
2. Add potatoes, chicken bouillon, water and parsley.
3. Add salt & pepper, to season.
4. Simmer for 20 minutes, or until potatoes become tender.
5. Mix flour and milk in a bowl, add to soup mixture & cook until soup thickens.
6. Incorporate the cheese, and ham.
7. Continue to simmer until cheese melts into the soup.

## Plate/Present

You can go two ways with this soup: Family style, or individual servings. Put the soup in a big turin, place it on a sideboard with some bowls and spoons, or if its more formal, you could ladle the soup into individual serving bowls, and garnish the top of the soup with some chopped basil, or even crumbled bacon bits.

Served in a cup, this soup makes a great addition to a meal. Served in a bowl with bread, it's a great meal that stands on its own.

## Tasty Additions

This recipe just begs for experimentation. For example, instead of cooked ham, you could substitute ground sirloin, or turkey. Or you could go vegetarian and leave out the meat completely, and substitute the chicken bullion with vegetable bullion.

As with any good soup, there should always be a loaf of good bread with a slab of butter on the side.

# Butternut Squash Soup

*Someone once said that soup is good food, and they were right. In the Fall and Winter months when the wind howls through the bare trees, and snow piles up in great drifts (I'm from Kansas), there is nothing like a nice hearty bowl of soup to warm you from head to toe. And squash is an excellent ingredient for just such a soup because it grows to maturity as the months move slowly toward Autumn.*

*This recipes goes great with a dollop of cranberry relish, or sour cream.*

## Prep/Prepare

1. Preheat the oven to 350 degrees F.
2. Cut each squash in half and discard the seeds. Brush cut sides with 2 tablespoons of melted butter, and then season with salt, pepper and nutmeg.
3. Arrange the squash cut side down on a rack placed in a baking tray and bake until tender, about 1 1/2 hours.
4. Cool, scoop out the insides of the squash, and puree the flesh in a food processor. Reserve. (You should have about 4 cups of pureed squash).
5. In a medium stock pot, melt the remaining 4 tablespoons of butter. Over low heat, sweat the onion. Do not allow them to brown.
6. Add the pureed squash and cook over very low heat until heated through, stirring occasionally.
7. Season with the salt, pepper, ginger, and cardamom.
8. Pour in the stock and bring to a boil, still over low heat, stirring often. Cook about 20 minutes.
9. In a small saucepan, heat the cream with the rosemary sprig. Remove the rosemary and pour the cream into the soup.
10. Transfer to a blender or food processor and process, in batches, for 2 or 3 minutes. Adjust the seasoning, to taste.

## Plate/Present

To serve, ladle the soup into heated bowls. Place a tablespoon of cranberry relish in the center, top with a dollop of cardamom cream, then sprinkle with chopped pecans. Drizzle pumpkin seed oil over soup.

If desired, bake small squash until tender, scoop out, and use as individual serving bowls.

## Plan/Purchase

### Ingredients

| | |
|---|---|
| 3 3/4 lb. | pumpkin or butternut squash |
| 1 | acorn squash (about 1 3/4 pounds) |
| 6 | T. (3/4 stick) unsalted butter |
| 1/2 | t. kosher salt |
| 1/8 | t. freshly ground white pepper |
| 1/4 | t. ground nutmeg |
| 1 | white onion (about 4 oz.), peeled, trimmed, and finely diced |
| 1/4 | t. ground ginger |
| 1/8 | t. ground cardamom |
| 4 | c. chicken stock or vegetable stock |
| 1 | c. heavy cream |
| 1 | sprig fresh rosemary |

### Chef's Tip

*This recipe uses butternut squash to incorporate a sweet flavor to the soup, and makes it an excellent way to end a cold Winter day.*

soup — Plan · Purchase · Prep · Prepare · Plate · Present

# Chicken Noodle Soup

What section on soups would be complete without a recipe for chicken noodle soup? And not just any chicken noddle soup, but one that's loaded with chicken flavor. Serve it during flu season, to your sick spouse. Or do what I do, pretend to get a sniffle, and make it just because it taste sooooo good.

The shift on this recipe is that you're going to use a game hen, in place of a whole chicken. The intense flavor of the hen really gives this soup its distinct flavor, so give it a try.

## Plan/Purchase

### Ingredients

| | |
|---|---|
| 5 | c. water |
| 3 | carrots, chopped |
| 1/4 | c. fresh parsley, chopped |
| 1 | sprig rosemary |
| 3 | stalks celery, chopped |
| 1/4 | t. ground black pepper |
| 1/4 | salt |
| 3 | slices fresh ginger root |
| 1/4 | t. cummin |
| 1 | Cornish game hen |
| 1 | c. egg noodles |

## Prep/Prepare

1. In a large pot over medium heat combine the, water, pepper, salt,, ginger, cumin, parsley, and rosemary. Add the hen and boil until hen is cooked, about 1 hour.
2. Remove the hen and allow to cool.
3. Remove the rosemary sprig, and the ginger slices from the broth.
4. Add the chopped carrots, and allow to simmer for fifteen minutes.
5. While the broth is simmering, remove the skin from the hen, and cut the flesh into bite size pieces.
6. Add the hen to the broth mixture, return to a boil, and then add the noodles.
7. Simmer for another 15 minutes, or until noodles are tender.

## Plate/Present

This is good old comfort food, so serve it up casual in plain bowls; with some crackers on the side.

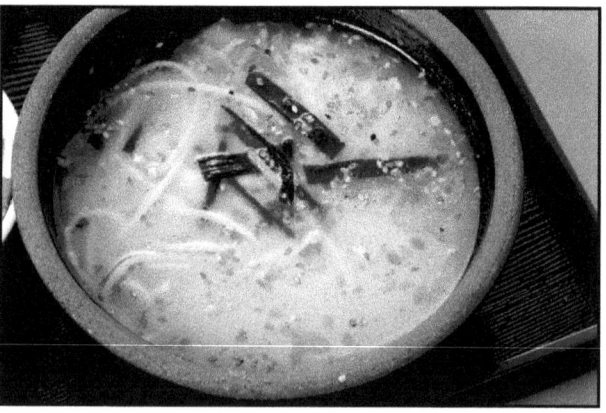

~ 140 ~

# Tomato Bisque with Basil

*This soup is a cold weather staple, but to be honest with you, I love this soup in any season. It's easy to make, tastes great, and it will definitely chase away the chill on a cold Winter day... soup is good food. Although using fresh ingredients is always the way to go, in most areas of the United States it might be a bit difficult to find fresh tomatoes during the Winter months, therefore canned tomatoes are acceptable, and if you use the right ones, it will be extremely difficult to taste the difference... HONEST.*

## Prep/Prepare

1. In a large pot, over medium heat, add the tomatoes and all the juices.
2. Stir in the bouillon, sugar, salt, bay leaf, basil, and pepper. Bring to a boil, then reduce heat and simmer for 30 minutes.
3. While the tomatoes are simmering, melt the butter in a small saucepan over medium heat, then whisk in all the flour to make a blond roux (see Appendix A: Roux).
4. When the roux thickens, add the milk a little at a time, cooking and stirring until thickened. Add this mixture to the simmering tomatoes and heat.

## Plate/Present

While not a necessity, serving this soup in a bread bowl, is a great homey touch. Most bakeries carry an assortment of small round loafs, just perfect for the occasion.

It might sound strange to use bouillon as opposed to stock (*I'm a big believer in home-made stocks and broths*); however, the bouillon helps to bring out the flavor of the tomatoes. If you happen to be using Knorr extra large cubes (*my favorite*), then use only one.

## What the recipe doesn't know

**Whether you're using fresh or canned tomatoes.** If you're using fresh tomatoes, then run them through a food mill to remove the seeds and skins. If using canned, add the entire contents of the can to the pot. And here's the kicker: Hunts Petite Diced canned tomatoes are awesome, and in many taste tests fooled even the experts (another excellent brand is Muir Glen Organic).

## Plan/Purchase

### Ingredients

| | |
|---|---|
| 2 | lb. tomatoes, diced |
| 2 | cubes beef bouillon |
| 1 | T. white sugar |
| 1 | t. salt |
| 1 | bay leaf |
| 1/4 | t. dried basil, or 1/2 t. fresh |
| 1/4 | t. ground black pepper |
| 4 | T. unsalted butter |
| 1/4 | c. all-purpose flour |
| 1 | pt. milk |

# French Onion Soup

French onion soup is an onion and beef broth based soup traditionally served with croutons and cheese as toppings. Although ancient in origin, this dish underwent a resurgence of popularity in the 1960s due to the growth of French cooking in the United States... Thank you, Julia Child.

This recipe keeps up the tradition, and tries to recreate the soup found in the small bistros and restaurants that line the winding streets of Paris.

## Plan/Purchase

### Ingredients

| | |
|---|---|
| 1/2 | c. unsalted butter |
| 2 | T. olive oil |
| 4 | c. sliced onions |
| 5 | c. beef broth |
| 2 | T. dry sherry (optional) |
| 1 | t. dried thyme |
| | salt and pepper to taste |
| 4 | slices French bread |
| 4 | slices provolone cheese |
| 2 | slices Swiss cheese, diced |
| 1/4 | c. grated Parmesan cheese |

## Prep/Prepare

1. Melt butter with olive oil in an 8 quart stock pot on medium heat. Add onions and continually stir until tender and translucent, and slightly brown.
2. Add beef broth, sherry & thyme.
3. Season with salt and pepper, and simmer for 30 minutes.
4. Turn on your oven broiler.
5. Add soup to oven-safe serving bowls, and place a slice of French bread on the top of each.
6. Top the bread with a slice of provolone, 1/2 slice diced Swiss and a tablespoon Parmesan cheese.
7. Place bowls on cookie sheet and broil until the cheese bubbles and browns slightly.

# Broccoli Soup

*Broccoli soup is one of those dishes that sneaks up on you. Most people wouldn't think much about this soup; however, once you've taken a bite you'll understand its charm.*

*If you have the time to make fresh chicken broth, then do it, because it will infuse the soup with intense, but not overpowering flavor. Additionally, I don't recommend using low-fat cheeses, because it will give the soup a flat, or missing something taste. As Julia Child might say, it you're worried about fat, eat smaller portions, but enjoy good flavor.*

## Prep/Prepare

1. Cut the broccoli florets from the stems, and discard the stems.
2. Bring broth to a boil.
3. Add broccoli and onion. Cook for five minutes, or until broccoli is tender.
4. In a separate bowl, slowly add milk to flour, and mix until well blended.
5. Stir flour mixture into broth mixture. Cook, stirring constantly, until soup is thick and bubbly.
6. Add cheese if desired; stir until melted. Add seasonings and serve.

## Chef's Tip

*Do not use pre-shredded cheese... in fact, never use pre-shredded cheese. It contains stabilizers that keep the cheese from clumping, and in most cases can throw off the flavors of a cheese-based soup.*

*So, get yourself a cheese grater, and get to work.*

## Plan/Purchase

### Ingredients

| | |
|---|---|
| 2 | c. chicken broth |
| 2 1/2 | c. fresh broccoli |
| 1/4 | c. chopped onion |
| 1 | c. milk |
| 2 | T. all-purpose flour |
| 1 | c. shredded Cheddar cheese (optional) |
| 1/2 | t. dried oregano |
| - | salt and pepper to taste |

### Chef's Tip

*Dried spices are usually more intense, so if using fresh, cut the amount by half.*

# Sandwiches
# Salads

The bread-enclosed convenience food known as the "sandwich" is attributed to John Montagu, fourth earl of Sandwich (1718–1792), a British statesman and notorious gambler, who is said to be the inventor of this type of food so that he would not have to leave his gaming table to take supper. In fact, Montagu was not the inventor of the sandwich; rather, during his excursions in the Eastern Mediterranean, he saw filled pita breads and small canapés and sandwiches served by the Greeks and Turks, and copied the concept for its obvious convenience. There is no doubt, however, that the Earl of Sandwich made this type of light repast popular among England's gentry, and in this way, his title has been associated with the sandwich ever since. The concept is supremely simple: delicate finger food is served between two slices of bread in a culinary practice of ancient origins among the Greeks and other Mediterranean peoples.

Literary references to sandwiches begin to appear in English during the 1760s, not only in connection with their presumed Englishness, but also under the assumption that they are a food consumed primarily by the masculine sex during late night drinking parties. This connotation does not change until the sandwich moves into general society as a supper food for late night balls and similar events toward the end of the eighteenth century.

During the nineteenth century, as midday dinner moved later and later into the day, the need for a hot supper declined, only to be replaced with light dishes made of cold leftovers, ingredients for which the sandwich proved preeminently suitable. Thus the sandwich became a fixture of intimate evening suppers, teas, and picnics, and popular fare for taverns and inns. This latter genre of sandwich has given rise to multitudes of working class creations, such as the butty and sarny of Britain, and the bacon-lettuce-and-tomato sandwich of the American diner.

# good eats

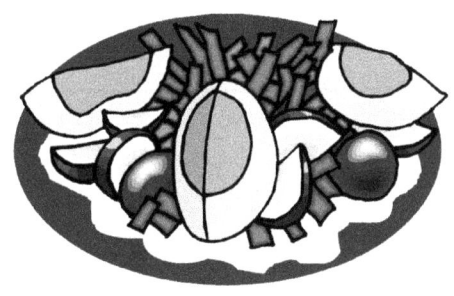

# Midnight Sandwiches

*This sandwich is a variation on what is know as a 'Media Noche', which translates to 'Midnight.' It makes a wonderful dinner sandwich because it is served hot. A nice side dish is black bean soup or black beans and rice.*

*Some chefs call this a Cuban Midnight Sandwich; however, that's inaccurate. Although some of the ingredients are similar, traditional Cuban Midnight sandwiches are made using roasted pork and topped with ham, no turkey, no mayo, and served on Cuban rolls.*

## Plan/Purchase

### Ingredients

| | |
|---|---|
| 1 | c. mayonnaise |
| 5 | T. Italian dressing |
| 4 | hoagie rolls split lengthwise |
| 4 | T. prepared mustard |
| 1/2 | lb. thinly sliced deli turkey meat |
| 1/2 | lb. thinly sliced cooked ham |
| 1/2 | lb. thinly sliced Swiss cheese |
| 1 | c. dill pickle slices |
| 1/2 | c. olive oil |

### Did You Know

*The traditional Cuban "Midnight" sandwich was assembled, and then lightly toasted in a sandwich press called a "plancha", very similar to a panini press, until the bread was crisp and the cheese melted... I don't know about you, but that sounds pretty tasty to me.*

## Prep/Prepare

1. In a small bowl, mix together mayonnaise and Italian dressing, and spread mixture on hoagie rolls. Then spread each roll with the mustard.
2. On each roll, arrange layers of turkey, ham, and cheese.
3. Top with dill pickle slices.
4. Close sandwiches, and brush tops and bottoms with olive oil.
5. Heat a non-stick skillet over medium high heat.
6. Place sandwiches in skillet, and cook for 2 minutes, pressing down with a large spatula.
7. Flip, and cook for 2 more minutes, or until cheese is melted.

## Plate/Present

Remove from heat, place on plates, and cut in half diagonally.

If you're feeling adventurous, you might want to add some sliced tomatoes and red onions.

For awesome presentation, the best type of pan to use for this sandwich is a panini pan and press. They're typically made of cast iron, and contain a grill-like surface. Included is a press (not a lid), that presses the food into the grill surface. This creates those lovely grill marks that we love to see. In addition, the press both heats and compresses the sandwich..

I prefer a panini pan and press to the dedicated panini presses you see advertised... The Pan is much easier to clean (by far), and can be used for things other than sandwiches; such as: grilled chicken breasts, or (without the press) grilled salmon.

# Tempting Tuna Salad

*I got this recipe from a friend of mine that absolutely loves tuna salad. She claims that she worked for years to get this recipe perfected, and I believe her. Two of the unusual ingredients are: curry and Parmesan cheese. But don't let that put you off, because whenever she serves this dish, her guests gobble it up, and always ask for the recipe.*

*Get some bread, or croissants, a bit of lettuce and tomato, and enjoy the meal.*

## Prep/Prepare

1. Combine the tuna, with the mayonnaise, Parmesan cheese, celery, relish and onion.
2. Season with curry, parsley, dill and garlic powder. Mix well.

## Plate/Present

If you can wait, cover and let rest in the refrigerator overnight. The rest really helps to blend the flavors.

If you can't wait, go for it.

Serve on fresh bakery bread with romaine lettuce, swiss cheese and a slice of garden-ripened tomato... this tuna is awesome.

## What the recipe doesn't know

**The type of tuna you're using.**

Several different varieties of tuna are canned. Skipjack, Bluefin and Yellowfin (called Ahi in Hawaii) tuna are canned and sold as "light meat," while Albacore (also called Longfin tuna, Tombo Ahi, and Ahi Palanacan) is the only tuna that can be labeled premium "white meat". Tuna is a source of omega 3 fats.

## Did You Know

To get the most omega 3 fats from your canned tuna, choose water-packed tuna rather than oil-packed. The oil mixes with some of the tuna's natural fat, so when you drain oil-packed tuna, some of its omega 3 fatty acids also go down the drain. Since oil and water don't mix, water-packed tuna won't leach any of its precious omega 3s.

## Plan/Purchase

### Ingredients

| | |
|---|---|
| 14 | oz. white tuna, drained and flaked |
| 6 | T. mayonnaise |
| 2 | T. Parmesan cheese |
| 5 | T. sweet pickle relish |
| 2 | T. diced onion |
| 2 | T. diced celery |
| 1/2 | t. curry powder |
| 2 | T. dried parsley |
| 2 | t. dried dill weed |
| 1/8 | t. garlic powder |

### Did You Know

Omega-3 fatty acids are a class of fatty acids found in fish oils, that act to lower the level of cholesterol and LDL (low-density lipoproteins) in the blood. (LDL cholesterol is the "bad" cholesterol.)

good eats — Plan - Purchase - Prep - Prepare - Plate - Present

# Roast Turkey Panini

*A panini or panino (singular) is a sandwich made from a small loaf of bread, typically a ciabatta. The loaf is often cut horizontally and filled with salami, ham, meat, cheese or other food, and served hot.*

*This particular sandwich uses savory smoked turkey, Italian seasoning, and a bit of cranberry sauce for the sweet. Cooked in a panini grill or pan using a press, this sandwich makes an excellent lunch or late-night snack.*

## Plan/Purchase

### Ingredients

| | |
|---|---|
| 1 | T. cream cheese, softened |
| - | Italian seasoning, to taste |
| 1 | large loaf ciabatta, cut in half lengthwise & then cut in half |
| 2 | T. whole cranberry sauce |
| 4 | oz. roasted turkey, sliced thin |
| 3 | thin slices red onion |
| - | freshly ground black pepper, to taste |
| 1 | T. butter |

## Prep/Prepare

1. Season cream cheese with a few dashes of Italian seasoning; spread on one slice of bread.
2. On the other bread slice, spread the cranberry sauce.
3. Layer the roasted turkey slices and onion on top of the cream cheese bread slice. Sprinkle with black pepper.
4. Lay the other slice (cranberry side down) on the top.
5. Lightly coat the top and bottom of the sandwich slices with butter.
6. Prepare a preheated panini pan with cooking spray, and place over medium heat.
7. Grill for 3 to 5 minutes or until the bread is golden brown.

## Plate/Present

Cut in half, on the diagonal, and serve hot

# Ham & Cheese Baguettes

Your typical ham & cheese sandwiches these ain't. These thin fingers of toasted bread, oozing with fresh ham and cheese make a great afternoon treat, or something to keep your guests satisfied before dinner. Alone they are a great nosh, combined with a salad or soup, they make for a great lunch or late-night treat.

The filling is a combination of shredded cheese, mustard, and Worcestershire... with a bit of sour cream for some kick, and to hold the whole thing together.

## Prep/Prepare

1. In a medium bowl, combine the cheese with the smoked ham, mustard, and Worcestershire sauce.
2. Mix well, then mix in the cream, adding just enough to form a firm mixture.
3. Spread the cheese and ham mixture thickly onto 4 pieces of the bread, top with the other 4 slices, and then press together.
4. Brush the outside of the bread with olive oil, or butter and brown over medium-high heat in a heavy skillet. Press lightly with your spatula as they cook (3 to 5 minutes).
5. Turn when light crisped, and then brown the second side (3 to 5 minutes).

## Plate/Present

The sandwiches should be served hot, right out of the pan.

You can cook the sandwiches in a panini pan, to give them a grilled appearance.

In addition, using a plain white plate, helps to set off the color of the sandwich.

As an appetizer, you can make up a whole bunch, put them on a plate, with small tea napkins on the side, and watch them disappear.

You could even serve them with a cup of tomato soup, or a small salad. This qualifies as a light lunch on the patio, or a late into-the-evening dinner/snack.

## What the recipe doesn't know

### The heat of your pan

The sandwich does not know the heat of your pan; therefore, the 3 to 5 minutes per side is simply a guideline. If you see the bread begin to brown, flip them over, regardless of the time.

## Plan/Purchase

### Ingredients

| | |
|---|---|
| 6 | oz. Gruyere or Emmentaler, or other Swiss cheese, shredded coarsely |
| 2-3 | oz. diced smoked ham |
| 1/2 | t. dry mustard |
| 1 | t. Worcestershire sauce |
| 1 | T. whipping cream, sour cream, or creme fresh |
| 8 | 1/2 inch slices from a long French baguette, cut on a slight diagonal |
| - | olive oil for brushing, or soft butter |

### Chef's Tip

Since the filling is so soft, the bread should be cut to the correct size before making the sandwiches; attempting to cut them after cooking will cause all the filling to ooze out... I hate it when that happens, and so will your guests.

good eats — Plan · Purchase · Prep · Prepare · Plate · Present

# Super Burgers with blue cheese

Don't write this burger off, just because it has blue cheese as an ingredient. As a matter of fact, the blue cheese really gives this burger its awesome flavor. If you're doing these babies on the grill, make sure to pre-heat, and clean the grill so that they don't stick, and so you don't pick up flavors from previous grilling experiences... I hate it when that happens.

These are great for inviting friends over on a warm Summer weekend. When the sun goes down, you might be able to catch some lightning bugs, and put them in a jar... just a thought.

## Plan/Purchase

### Ingredients

| | |
|---|---|
| 3 | lb. lean ground beef |
| 4 | oz. blue cheese, crumbled |
| 1/2 | c. minced fresh chives |
| 1/4 | t. hot pepper sauce |
| 1 | t. Worcestershire sauce |
| 1 | t. coarsely ground black pepper |
| 1.5 | t. salt |
| 1 | t. dry mustard |

### Chef's Tip

To prevent the burgers from rising up in the middle (called doming), place a patty on a flat surface and use your thumb to create an indentation in the middle. That leaves the edges of the burger slightly fatter than the middle (something like a donut).

When you cook the burger it will contract, and as it contracts, the middle will fill back out.

Without this technique, many cooks will press on the burger with their spatula to push the middle back down, and in doing so, lose the great juices and flavor.

~ 150 ~

## Prep/Prepare

1. Mix all the ingredients together in a large bowl, but don't over mix.
2. Place the bowl in the refrigerator, covered, for a minimum of 2 hours.
3. Divide the burger into twelve balls, and form into patties. This will make 1/4 pound burgers.
4. Clean, your grill and preheat for medium high (see Appendix A: Grill Temperature, and Grill Cleaning).
5. Cook the patties to your liking (5 minutes per side, for well done).

## Plate/Present

These hamburgers go great on crusty bread, such as French bread. Brush with butter, and lay on the grill to toast.

Good sides would be corn on the cob, grilled potatoes, and a side salad.

Cooking with a Plan Vol I: Back to the Kitchen                good eats

# Not So Boring Potato Salad

*Potato salad is a dish made from potatoes, and varies throughout different regions and countries of the world. With respect to its place among the various individual menu courses served together as one meal, it is better classified as a side dish rather than a salad*

*This is definitely not your typical, bring-to-the-BBQ potato salad. I recommend that before you try your own variation, you should make it by the recipe... you'll love it.*

## Prep/Prepare

1. Bring a large pot of water to a boil. Add potatoes and cook until tender but still firm, 10 to 15 minutes.
2. Lay the potatoes on a baking sheet, and sprinkle with the chopped dill, and vinegar. Set aside and allow to cool.
3. Boil the eggs (see Appendix A: Boiling Eggs), then cool, peel, and chop.
4. Cook the bacon until brown and crisp, then cool, drain, crumble and set aside.
5. Place the cooled potatoes in a large bowl, and then add the eggs, bacon, onion and celery.
6. Finally, add the mayonnaise, salt and pepper to taste.
7. Chill for at least 2 hours in a covered bowl.

## Plan/Purchase

### Ingredients

| | |
|---|---|
| 2 | lb. red potatoes, cleaned and cut into bite size pieces |
| 2 | T. chopped fresh dill |
| 3 | T. red wine vinegar |
| 6 | eggs |
| 1 | lb. bacon |
| 1 | onion, finely chopped |
| 1 | stalk celery, finely chopped |
| 2 | c. mayonnaise |
| - | salt and pepper, to taste |

~ 151 ~

good eats — Plan · Purchase · Prep · Prepare · Plate · Present

# Grilled Veggie Sandwich

*I found this great tasting sandwich while on a trip to San Francisco, and managed to get the recipe from the restaurant chef. Since we have a lot of vegetarian friends, this is a great sandwich to serve them at an afternoon BBQ. However, don't let the all-veggie recipe fool you, this baby tastes great whether you're a meat-eater (like me), or a vegetarian... guaranteed.*

*Just grill it up and see if you don't agree that's it's one tasty sandwich.*

## Plan/Purchase

### Ingredients

| | |
|---|---|
| 1/4 | c. mayonnaise |
| 3 | cloves garlic, minced |
| 1 | plum tomato, sliced |
| 1 | T. lemon juice |
| 1/8 | c. olive oil |
| 1 | c. red bell peppers, sliced |
| 1 | small zucchini, sliced |
| 1 | red onion, sliced |
| 1 | small yellow squash, sliced |
| 2 | (4-x6-inch) focaccia bread pieces, cut open. |
| 1/2 | c. crumbled feta cheese |

### Alternate Method

*If you don't want to use the grill because there's three feet of snow on the ground, and the grill is buried in a snow drift, you can use the broiler for the veggies, and warm the focaccia in the oven.*

## Prep/Prepare

1. Combine the mayonnaise, garlic, and lemon juice in a small bowl, and then set covered in the refrigerator.
2. Clean, your grill and preheat for high (see Appendix A: Grill Temperature, and Grill Cleaning).
3. Put the olive oil in a bowl, and toss vegetables to evenly coat.
4. Cook the veggies until tender and have grill marks (about 3 to 5 minutes per side). Set aside.
5. Spread the mayonnaise mixture on the cut sides of the focaccia, and then sprinkle with feta cheese.
6. Place bread on the grill cheese side up, cover the grill, and let set for 2 or 3 minutes. This will warm the bread, and slightly melt the cheese. Cheese should be slightly melted.
7. Remove bread from grill.

## Plate/Present

This is an open face sandwich, so the 2 pieces of focaccia produce 4 sandwiches.

Place one of the focaccia pieces on a plate and then layer with 1/4 of the grilled veggies.

## Additions

For a topping, as if this dish needs a topping, I like to saute some mixed mushrooms in butter, and add them to the sandwich at the end.

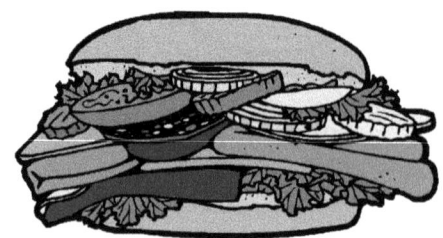

*Cooking with a Plan Vol 1: Back to the Kitchen*  *good eats*

# Pulled Beef Sandwiches

*Oh, your guests are going to love you for this one. When I make it I never have any leftovers, and I'm always asked for the recipe. It takes a bit of time to make; however, the results are well worth the time.*

*I know 8 hours is a lot of prep; however, you're not spending it all in the kitchen. As a matter of fact, the roast does just fine simmering all by its lonesome.*

## *Prep/Prepare*

1. Mix the water and broth together.
2. Place the roast in a large pot and cover with the water/broth mixture.

**Note: Depending on the roast and the size of your pot, you may need more, or less of the liquid.**

3. Mix in bouillon, salt, and garlic salt.

**Note: If you are not using low sodium broth, reduce the salt to 1 teaspoon.**

4. Create a pouch out of cheese cloth, insert the bay leaves, peppercorns, and rosemary and securely tie with some kitchen twine (called a Bouquet Garni).
5. Add this to the pot, and tie the end of the twine to the pot handle (this will make it easier to find and remove later).
6. Bring the roast to a boil using high heat
7. Reduce to low heat, cover with a tight fitting lid, and simmer for 6 to 8 hours. The roast will be fork tender.
8. Remove Bouquet Garni and discard.
9. Remove roast from the pot and shred ( a good way to do this is by using two forks).
10. Reserve the flavorful broth for dipping.

## *Plate/Present*

This sandwich just cries out for crusty rolls of French bread, and bowls for the dipping sauce.

## *Tasty Additions*

About two hours into the cooking process, add some cut carrots, red potatoes, and a quartered onion. Not only will this help to flavor the broth, but the veggies are great as a side dish.

## *Plan/Purchase*

### Ingredients

| | |
|---|---|
| 5 | lb. chuck roast |
| 2 | c. beef broth |
| 2 | c. water |
| 2 | T. salt |
| 2 | t. garlic salt |
| 2 | bay leaves |
| 1.5 | t. fresh rosemary (you can substitute dry, if needed) |
| 2 | T. black or green peppercorns, whole |

### *Chef's Tip*

*If you don't want to leave something on the stove for 5 or 6 hours, you can set the rack in your oven to the lower position, and preheat to 250° f.*

*After the roast comes to a boil on the stove, cover and place in the oven. It will still take 5 or 6 hours of time, but the results will essentially be the same.*

*Just make sure you're using an oven-proof pot.*

# Classic Caesar Salad

Caesar Salad [SEE-zer] consists of greens (classically, romaine lettuce) tossed with a garlic vinaigrette dressing (made with worcestershire sauce and lemon juice), grated Parmesan cheese, croutons, a coddled egg and sometimes anchovies. It is said to have been created in 1924 by Italian chef Caesar Cardini, who owned a restaurant in Tijuana, Mexico.

The two things that are controversial are the use of raw or coddled egg, and the anchovy fillets. As you can see the recipe has no egg, and if you like you can leave out the anchovy fillets.

## Plan/Purchase

### Ingredients

| | |
|---|---|
| 6 | cloves garlic, peeled |
| 3/4 | c. mayonnaise |
| 5 | anchovy fillets, minced |
| 6 | T. grated Parmesan cheese, divided |
| 1 | t. Worcestershire sauce |
| 1 | t. Dijon mustard |
| 1 | T. lemon juice |
| - | salt to taste |
| - | ground black pepper to taste |
| 1/4 | c. olive oil |
| 6 | slices of day-old bread, cubed, about 4 cups |
| 1 | romaine lettuce head, hand torn into bite-size pieces |

## Prep/Prepare

1. Mince 3 of the garlic cloves, and the anchovy fillets (if using).
2. In the small bowl of a blender or food processor, add the mayonnaise, garlic, anchovies, 2 tablespoons of Parmesan cheese, Worcestershire sauce, mustard, and lemon juice. Blend until smooth. Season with salt and pepper, and then cover and refrigerate until needed.
3. Cut the other 3 garlic cloves in half.
4. Heat the olive oil in a large skillet over medium heat, add the garlic and saute until the garlic begins to turn brown.
5. Remove and discard the garlic.

**Note: Do not let the garlic burn, or it will overpower the croutons.**

6. Add the bread cubes to the hot oil, and cook, until lightly browned.
7. Remove croutons from oil, and season lightly with salt and pepper, if desired.

## Plate/Present

Place lettuce in a large bowl, retrieve the dressing from the refrigerator, and toss with the lettuce

As a final step, top with the remaining Parmesan cheese, and croutons.

# Mandarin Orange, Spring Salad

*This is an excellent salad on a Spring day, it's super easy to fix, and the blending of the mandarin oranges with the cheese make for a wonderful experience for your palette.*

*A lot of people never get the flavor connection between cheese and fruit, but if you've never tried the combination, now is a good time to start. As a matter of fact, if you have an apple lying around, and a bit of sharp cheddar, cut off a slice of the apple with the cheese... I think you'll enjoy it.*

## Prep/Prepare

1. Heat a dry skillet over medium-high heat, and then add the almonds,
2. Stir often, until lightly toasted and fragrant. Place in a small bowl and set aside.
3. Whisk the mandarin juice, orange juice, oil, and vinegar, in a small bowl, until fully incorporated.

## Plate/Present

Toss the toasted almonds, mandarin oranges, salad greens, and Gorgonzola cheese in a big bowl.

Add the dressing, just before serving, pour on the salad, and lightly toss to coat.

## Plan/Purchase

### Ingredients

- 1/2 c. slivered almonds
- 3 mandarin oranges, peeled and separated into wedges
- 1 fresh orange, peeled and separated into wedges

Reserve one or two of the mandarin and orange wedges, squeeze and reserve the juice You should have 2 tablespoons of orange, and mandarin juice.

- 2 T. vegetable oil
- 2 T. red wine vinegar
- 12 oz. salad greens, spring mix
- 3/4 c. Gorgonzola cheese

### Chef's Tip

If you can't find fresh mandarin oranges, you can always use canned. The size of the can should be about 14 ounces.

~ 155 ~

# Stocks, Broths, Sauces

## Stock

A flavored liquid, forming the basis of many dishes, particularly soups and sauces.

Stock is prepared by simmering various ingredients in water, such as: a combination of onions, carrots, celery, and sometimes other vegetables.

Often the less desirable parts of the vegetables (such as carrot skins and celery ends) are used since they will not be eaten.

Herbs and spices are used depending on availability and local traditions. In classical cuisine, the use of a bouquet garni (or bundle of herbs) consisting of parsley, bay leaves, a sprig of thyme and possibly other herbs, is common. This is often wrapped in a cheesecloth "bag" and tied with string to make it easier to remove it once the stock is cooked.

Added to this mix would be some chicken parts, beef, or fish, depending on the type of stock desired.

## Broth

A liquid in which bones, meat, fish, cereal grains, or vegetables have been simmered and strained out.

Broth is used as a basis for other edible liquids such as soup, gravy, or sauce. It can be eaten alone or with garnish.

U.S. culinary schools often differentiate between broth, usually made from viable portions of animal meat, and stock, which may be less palatable, often made from vegetable scraps and bones.

Broth has been made for many years using the bones of animals. Traditionally bones are boiled in a cooking pot for long periods extracting the flavor and nutrients from the bones. The bones may or may not have meat still on them.

In East Asia (particularly Japan), a form of kelp called kombu is often used as the basis for broths (called dashi in Japanese).

# the liquids of life

## Sauce

A liquid or sometimes semi-solid food served on or used in preparing other foods. Sauces are not consumed by themselves; they add flavor, moisture, and visual appeal to another dish. Sauce is a French word taken from the Latin salsus, meaning salted. Sauces need a liquid component, but with dishes such as pasta can contain more solid elements than liquid.

Sauces may be prepared sauces, such as soy sauce, which are usually bought, not made, by the cook; or cooked sauces, such as Béchamel sauce, which are generally made just before serving. Sauces for salads are called salad dressing. Another variation is the pan sauce; this is made by adding an aromatic (such as chopped shallot) to a pan that has previously cooked meat, which has left hardened juices (called the fond) in the pan. After the aromatic has softened, a liquid (such as stock, wine, or water) is added to melt the fond in the bottom of the pan (a process called deglazing). Butter can than be added to this to make a quick sauce.

A person who specializes in making sauces is often referred to as a "saucier", a French term borrowed for its situational usefulness. Sauces are an essential element in cuisines all over the world.

everything else | Plan · Purchase · Prep · Prepare · Plate · Present

# Chunky Cherry Tomato Sauce

*This is an excellent sauce to use with just about any type of fish. The lemon juice adds just the right amount of birghtness to the sauce without overpowering the fish.*

*And, as you can see, the recipe is deceptively simple to make... just tomatoes and a few other odds and ends, marinating in a bowl. No cooking, or baking, just great taste.*

*You can even use this recipe on some Summer greens, fresh from the garden.*

## Plan/Purchase

### Ingredients

| | |
|---|---|
| 1/2 | pint cherry or grape tomatoes, each tomato quartered (about 1 cup) |
| 1/4 | t. salt |
| 1/4 | t. ground black pepper |
| 2 | medium shallots, minced (about 3 tablespoons) |
| 2 | T. minced fresh basil leaves |
| 3 | T. juice from 1 lemon |
| 6 | T. extra-virgin olive oil |

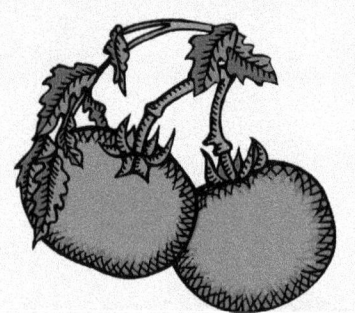

## Prep/Prepare

1. Mix tomatoes with salt and pepper in medium mixing bowl; let stand until juicy and seasoned, about 10 minutes.
2. Whisk shallots, basil, lemon juice, and oil in small mixing bowl; add to tomatoes and toss to combine.

## Chef's Tip

This dish goes great over mixed greens, or use it to compliment your favorite grilled or pan-fried fish.

Cooking with a Plan Vol I: Back to the Kitchen  everything else

# Homemade Chicken Stock

*Nothing beats homemade chicken stock. You've got your bullion cubes, and cans of chicken stock; however, nothing quite beats the taste of making your own, from scratch... honest. This recipe takes most of the day, but the results are worth the efforts. As a matter of fact, after you've skimmed off the fat and impurities that come to the surface (about an hour), all you need to do is let is slowly simmer and do its thing.*

## Prep/Prepare

1. Place all the ingredients into a large (3 to 4 gallon) stockpot and set over a medium-high heat. Bring the contents of the pot to a boil and reduce to a simmer.
2. Skim the impurities and fat that rise to the top.
3. Simmer the stock about 1 hour, skimming as needed. Do not allow the stock to boil, or the fat and scum will mix with the stock and cause it to become cloudy.
4. After one hour, remove the chicken from the pot, let cool slightly, then remove the meat from the bones, and reserve for another use, like a chicken salad, or a soup, gumbo or ragout
5. Return the bones to the pot and slowly simmer for another 4 or 5 hours.
6. When the stock is complete remove the bones, and strain the liquid through a fine mesh sieve or china cap lined with cheesecloth.
7. Refrigerate or freeze what is not used (lasts up to 4 months frozen).

## Chef's Tip

It's very important that you spend time up front with the stock, skimming off the impurities and fat that rise to the top. Use a small slotted spoon, or strainer to remove the offensive material and discard down the drain.

If done correctly, you'll be rewarded with a clear (not cloudy) stock.

## What the recipe doesn't know

**Your definition of a simmer.**

Since this recipe calls for a long simmering time (5 hours), a slight variation in temperature can totally change your stock. Remember, it's a slow simmer... that means that the small bubbles break before reaching the surface.

## Plan/Purchase

### Ingredients

| | |
|---|---|
| 2 | (3 1/2 to 4 lb.) chickens, well rinsed, quartered with the excess fat removed |
| 2 | gal. cold water, or enough to cover the chickens |
| 2 | c. coarsely chopped onions |
| 1 | c. coarsely chopped carrots |
| 1 | c. coarsely chopped celery |
| 1/4 | c. peeled garlic |
| - | salt, to taste |
| 1 | Bouquet Garni* |

### Bouquet Garni*

*Consisting of: 2 bay leaves, 1/4 teaspoon dried thyme, 1/4 teaspoon cracked black peppercorns, 4 parsley stems, wrapped in cheesecloth and tied with string.*

### Chef's Tip

*Freeze some of the additional stock using an ice tray, and then place the cubes in a resealable plastic bag. That way, when you need a bit more stock for a sauce, stew or béchamel, all you have to do is grab a cube.*

### Did You Know

*The gelatin from the chicken bones is released during the long cooking time yielding a rich, flavorful stock.*

everything else — Plan · Purchase · Prep · Prepare · Plate · Present

# Building a Raft

Okay, you're on the deserted island with Gilligan and crew (I had a crush on Mary Ann). You decide that the only way off the island is the construction of a raft. Well, that's not the kind of raft we're referring to in this section. A raft is basically a mixture of ingredients used to clarify a consomme. If you go to the Culinary Institute you will have to master this technique in the first three weeks of school.

Believe me, the clear broth that it creates is well worth the effort.

## Plan/Purchase

### Ingredients

- 5 egg whites
- 1 1/4 lb. ground chicken thighs
- 1 tomato, chopped
- 1 t. kosher salt
- 3/4 c. finely chopped onion
- 1/3 c. finely chopped leek
- 2/3 c. finely chopped celery
- 6 parsley stems
- 1 bay leaf
- 3 springs thyme
- 1/2 clove garlic
- 6 peppercorns
- 1 1/2 qt. cold chicken stock

### Chef's Note

The results are amazing... you'll begin with a cloudy chicken stock, and end up with crystal clear stock. Several soups and consommes require (for presentation) a clear stock. Clear stocks show off the other items in the soup; like the veggies.

For example, a great presentation for tortilla soup is using clear broth to show off the veggies and meat.

## Prep/Prepare

1. In medium bowl, whisk together egg whites, onion, carrot, celery and tomato until slightly frothy. Mix in ground chicken.
2. Place cloudy chicken stock in medium saucepan and whisk mixture into stock. Bring to slow simmer while constantly stirring in one direction with wooden spoon.
3. Stir for about 15 minutes or until raft—a fairly solid layer on top of liquid—begins to form. Reduce to slow simmer and stop stirring.
4. After raft forms, break a small hole in the center to allow consomme to break through. Continue to simmer for 45 minutes or until liquid appears crystal clear.
5. Strain through fine-mesh strainer lined with cheesecloth, being careful not to break raft.
6. Discard raft and season consomme with salt and pepper.

Cooking with a Plan Vol 1: Back to the Kitchen                              everything else

# Pineapple Reduction

*In cooking, a reduction is the process of thickening or intensifying the flavor of a liquid mixture, such as a soup, sauce, wine, or juice by evaporation. Common preparations involving reductions include: consommés, reduced and clarified stocks, gravies, pan sauces, and syrups.*

*This particular reduction gives you a pineapple sauce that's just bursting with flavor. This recipe is an excellent sauce for use on a grilled chicken breast, or a firm white fish.*

*You have to give this one a try... you'll love it.*

## Prep/Prepare

1. Melt butter in small sauté pan until bubbling.
2. Add the red pepper flakes, pineapple dice, and sake.
3. Slowly cook down in an uncovered pan, until the liquid has almost evaporated.

## Plate/Present

This reduction will spice up a plain piece of chicken or fish in a flash, and it's also great when spooned over a plate of long-grain steamed white rice.

Give it a try, but watch out for those red pepper flakes, they can deliver quite a kick.

## Plan/Purchase

### Ingredients

| | |
|---|---|
| 1 | **whole ripe pineapple, diced** |
| 1 | **t. unsalted butter** |
| 1 | **T. crushed red pepper** |
| 4 | **T. sake** |

### Chef's Note

*The red pepper flakes are what give this reduction its kick. However, red pepper gives quite a big kick. If you're not a big fan of hot, hot, hot, you might want to reduce the flakes by half.*

everything else — Plan · Purchase · Prep · Prepare · Plate · Present

# Butter-Sage Sauce

People always ask the question: Does the sauce make the dish? A sauce should never overpower the dish. In cooking, a sauce is a liquid served on or used in the preparation of food. Sauces are not consumed by themselves; they add flavor, moisture, and visual appeal to the dish.

The word sauce is a French word taken from the Latin *salsus*, meaning salted. Remember, if all you can taste is the sauce, then you've gone to far.

## Plan/Purchase

### Butter Sage Sauce

| | |
|---|---|
| 1 | T. shallots, minced |
| 1/4 | c. white wine |
| 1/4 | c. chicken broth |
| 3 | T. lemon juice, freshly squeezed |
| 7 | T. butter |
| 1 | t. fresh sage leaves, minced |

### Chef's Tip

There are a lot of white wines on the market... including cooking wines. The rule of thumb in choosing a wine to cook with is simply this: If you wouldn't drink it, then don't cook with it.

~ 162 ~

## Prep/Prepare

1. Preheat (medium high) a sauté pan, add 1 tablespoon of butter, add minced shallots and then sauté until soft (1 to 2 minutes).
2. Add the wine to deglaze the pan, and stir to combine.
3. Continue over high heat until nearly evaporated.
4. Add chicken broth and lemon juice, and reduce by half (3 minutes).
5. Remove from heat and swirl in 2 tablespoons of butter at a time,
6. Add another 2 tablespoons of butter, only after the last has incorporated into the sauce.
7. Finish by adding the sage.

**Note: Do not add the butter while the sauce is boiling, or it will separate.**

## Plate/Present

This sauce goes great with chicken; including the fantastic Saltimbocca recipe in the poultry section.

# Thyme and Red Pepper Cream

*This thyme and red pepper cream serves several functions; it can be used to decorate and spice soups (like the garlic soup in the soup section), or it can be placed into squeeze bottles, and used to create decorative patterns on serving plates. Since this recipe uses cream, and is not simply a vegetable or fruit puree, it has a limited shelf life that can be measured in hours... not days.*
*So make it the day you need it... and use it all up.*

## Prep/Prepare

1. Remove the skin, stem, and seeds from the peppers (See Appendix A: Skinning a Pepper).
2. Push the pepper through a heavy-duty sieve into a bowl and set aside. This will create a pepper puree.
3. Whisk the cream in a bowl until it holds very soft peaks but is not too stiff (you could use a mechanical, or electric beater). With a rubber spatula, fold half of the cream into the pepper puree, add 1/2 teaspoon of the lemon juice, and then season with salt and pepper.
4. In a separate bowl, stir the thyme and remaining 1/2 teaspoon lemon juice into the rest of the cream, and then season with salt and pepper.
5. Use immediately or cover and refrigerate the two creams separately for up to 3 hours.
6. Note: This will give you two sauces, one red pepper, and one thyme. Each one has it's own distinct color, and taste.

## Plate/Present

Put each of the creams into separate squeeze bottles. You can find them at almost any store. As a matter of fact, they look like the old squeeze bottles for ketchup and mustard, that you see in restaurants.

Then you can use them for the decoration of a serving dish, or to create cool patterns in a bowl of soup.

## Plan/Purchase

### Ingredients

| | |
|---|---|
| 1 | red bell pepper |
| 2 | t. olive oil |
| 1/2 | C. heavy cream |
| 1 | t. freshly squeezed lemon juice |
| 1 | t. chopped thyme leaves |
| | **Kosher salt** |
| | **Freshly ground black pepper** |

### Chef's Tip

*Remember, this recipe creates two separate creams. So, after whipping the cream, have two bowls, and place half the cream in each bowl. Then fold the pepper puree into one bowl of cream, and the thyme into the other.*

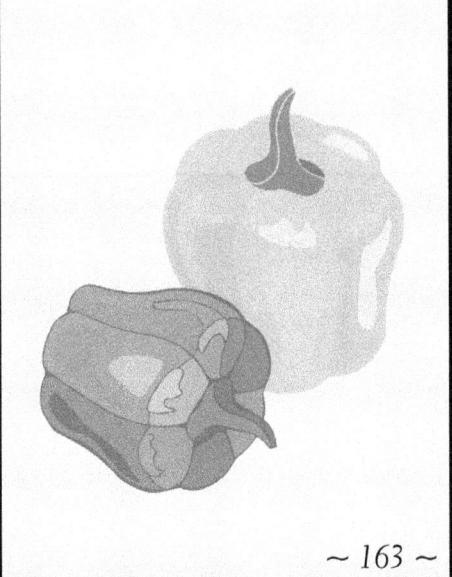

*everything else*   Plan · Purchase · Prep · Prepare · Plate · Present

# Classic Marinara

Marinara is a basic Italian tomato sauce. As a matter of fact, my concept of a marinara was some tomatoes (probably canned) simmered with some seasoning; that's until I went to school with my Aunt Josephine who taught be the absolute best marinara, straight from her home town of Naples.

Don't let the simplicity of the recipe fool you, it's got great tomato flavor.

Now, whenever I make a Marinara, this is the recipe I use... thanks Aunt Josephine, you're the best.

## Plan/Purchase

### Ingredients

| | |
|---|---|
| 1/4 | c. extra virgin olive oil |
| 1 | c. spanish onion, minced |
| 1 | T. garlic, minced |
| 6 | c. roma tomatoes, peeled, seeded, & diced |
| 1/4 | T. fresh basil, chiffonade |
| - | salt/pepper, to taste |

### Chef's Tip

Since the cooking time on this sauce is minimal, the onion and garlic should be cut into small pieces... that will help to quickly incorporate them into the sauce.

~ 164 ~

## Prep/Prepare

1. Remove the skins and seeds from the tomatoes, and then dice (See Appendix A: Blanching & Seeding Tomatoes).
2. Mince the onion and garlic.
3. Heat the olive oil in a saute pan over medium high heat, until it begins to shimmer.
4. Add the onion and continue to stir until transparent.
5. Add the garlic and cook until you can smell it. This will only take about 30 seconds.
6. Add the tomatoes, reduce the heat to medium, and simmer uncovered until the tomatoes lose their bright red color, about 20 minutes.
7. While the tomatoes are cooking, chiffonade the basil (See Appendix A: Chiffonade).
8. Remove pan from heat, add the basil, and then salt and pepper, to taste.

## Plate/Present

Serve over a bed of your favorite pasta, and cover with some freshly grated Parmigiano-Reggiano.

## Additions

Now that you've got this great marinara, why not try adding a few things, like some meatballs, or make a seafood marinara with shrimp, mussels, & clams.

Have some fun, experiment and enjoy yourself.

# Flavorful Beef Stock

*They say that good things come to those who wait, and this is no exception. The hour to cook the veggies and bones, along with the five hours of simmer time, make a great beef stock, that you will never be able to duplicate with a can, box, or cube.*

*Take it from me, once you start making your own stocks and broths, you'll never settle for anything else. As a matter of fact, with the amount of time it takes to make this stock, you just might want to double the recipe, and freeze some... it will keep for several months in the freezer.*

## Prep/Prepare

1. Adjust the rack in your oven to the middle position, and preheat to 425° f.
2. Place the soup bones in a large baking dish, and then scatter onions and carrots around the dish.
3. Bake, uncovered, until the bones are well browned (about 1 hour). Use a pair of tongs to turn the veggies and bones. Do this 2 or 3 times.
4. Drain the fat and reserve for another cooking project.
5. Place bones, onion, and carrots into a large soup pot. Then pour in about 1/2 cup of water into the roasting pan and mix with the remaining bits stuck to the bottom of the pan, and pour this liquid into soup pot.
6. Add the 12 cups water, and the rest of the veggies to the pot.
7. Bring the mixture to a boil, then reduce the heat. Cover and simmer for 5 hours.
8. Discard meat, vegetables, and seasonings, and then strain the stock through a china cap, or sieve lined with cheesecloth.

## Chef's Tip

Stocks and broths, made in this manner are typically cloudy. If you want clear stock, sometimes referred to as a consommé, see Raft Building in Appendix A.

## Plan/Purchase

### Ingredients

| | |
|---|---|
| 6 | lb. beef soup bones |
| 1 | large yellow onion, cut into 1/2 slices |
| 3 | large carrots, cut into 1 inch pieces |
| 1/2 | c. water |
| 2 | stalks celery, including some leaves, cut into 1 inch slices |
| 1 | large tomato, diced |
| 1/2 | c. parsnip, chopped |
| 1/2 | c. cubed potatoes |
| 8 | black peppercorns, whole |
| 4 | fresh parsley sprigs |
| 1 | bay leaf |
| 1 | T. salt |
| 2 | t. dried thyme |
| 2 | cloves garlic |
| 12 | c. water |

### Chef's Tip

*When you make your own stock, you can control the sodium. I usually cut the salt to 1/4 teaspoon, and add more later, when I'm using the stock in a recipe.*

everything else — Plan · Purchase · Prep · Prepare · Plate · Present

# Down Home BBQ Sauce

There are probably as many BBQ sauces out there, as there are chefs making them. However, once you taste this sauce, you're going to wonder why you ever bought one of those bottled versions.

Once made it can be bottled and stored in the refrigerator for several weeks. Then any time you need a bit of BBQ sauce for the impromptu outdoors gathering... bingo, you've got what you need to make the party Zing. Just remember, don't apply BBQ sauce as you're grilling. If applied too early, the sugars will burn, giving the sauce a bitter taste

## Plan/Purchase

### Ingredients

| | |
|---|---|
| 1/2 | onion, minced |
| 4 | c. cloves garlic, minced |
| 3/4 | c. bourbon whiskey |
| 1/2 | t. ground black pepper |
| 1/2 | T. salt |
| 2 | c. ketchup |
| 1/4 | c. tomato paste |
| 1/3 | c. cider vinegar |
| 2 | T. liquid smoke flavoring |
| 1/4 | c. Worcestershire sauce |
| 1/2 | c. packed brown sugar |
| 1/3 | t. hot pepper sauce, or to taste |

## Prep/Prepare

1. Combine the onion, garlic, and whiskey in a skillet over medium heat. Simmer for about 10 minutes, or until the onion is translucent.
2. Add the ground black pepper, salt, ketchup, tomato paste, vinegar, liquid smoke, Worcestershire sauce, brown sugar, and hot pepper sauce, and bring to a boil.
3. Reduce to medium-low, and simmer for 20 minutes.
4. Run sauce through a strainer if you prefer a smooth sauce.

*Cooking with a Plan Vol I: Back to the Kitchen*     *everything else*

# Awesome Alfredo Sauce

*Here's the myth... Fettuccine Alfredo became extremely popular, and di Lelio's restaurant attracted many celebrities. Two of these were Mary Pickford and Douglas Fairbanks, who fell in love with the dish while on their honeymoon in 1927, and gave him a golden fork to serve it... so the story goes.*

*Alfredo has now become ubiquitous in Italian-American restaurants in the United States, though in Italy, it is mostly served to American tourists. This recipe is a bit different because of the addition of cream cheese. This might sound strange; however, it makes for one awesome sauce.*

## Prep/Prepare

1. In a medium saucepan, melt the butter, over medium heat.
2. Add the garlic powder, combine, and then add the cream cheese, and then whisk until smooth.
3. Slowly incorporate the milk, and whisk until smooth.
4. Add the Parmesan cheese and pepper.
5. Stir until the sauce thickens, and then remove from the heat.

## Plate/Present

As a sauce it goes well with any pasta dish. It should be served right after making.

## Plan/Purchase

### Ingredients

| | |
|---|---|
| 1/2 | c. butter (unsalted) |
| 8 | oz. cream cheese at room temperature |
| 2 | t. garlic powder |
| 2 | c. milk |
| 6 | oz. grated Parmesan cheese |
| 1/8 | t. black pepper (ground) |

### Chef's Tip

*Alfredo sauce is sold today as a convenience food in many grocery stores around the country. Unlike the original preparation, which is thickened only by cheese, this is thickened with starch. Therefore, avoid the store-bought variety and always make it from scratch.*

# Appendix A

This part of Cooking with a Plan is designed to give you explanations and tips on the most commonly used cooking techniques, from boiling and blanching to whipping; including stewing, grilling, sauté, freezing, roasting, poaching and many more.

And no matter whether you are a novice in the kitchen or an experienced cook, this guide will be useful, because learning never stops.

# Techniques

# Appendix A

## Beans

Soaking lets the beans absorb water and softens their tough skins, and this results in a more even cooking and a shorter cooking time. As a rule, first rinse the beans in cold water to remove dust and any debris or wrinkled beans that float to the surface. Then place the beans in a bowl or container and cover them with two inches of cold water. Soak them overnight, at least 6-8 hours, and even longer for some varieties. If you cannot soak the beans in advance, a "quick" method can be used. Place the beans in a large pot and cover them with two inches of water. After bringing the beans to a boil, turn off the heat, cover them, and let them soak for one hour. Quick soaked beans will take longer to cook. In both cases, the beans are ready to be cooked as directed, or you can drain and store them in the refrigerator for a number of days.

## Blanching & Seeding Tomatoes

Most tomato sauce recipes call for the skinning and seeding of the tomatoes. To remove the skins, bring a pot of water to the boil. Meanwhile cut a small X into the bottom of the tomatoes, and place in the boiling water for about 30 seconds. Remove the tomatoes and drop into a bowl of ice water. The skins should slid off with little effort. To seed the tomato, cut them in half, take a small spoon, and scoop out the seeds, or you could use your hand to gently squeeze the seeds into sink.

While the skin of a tomato is fine for things like salads, it will not incorporate into sauces, and the seeds, if left in, will impart a bitter taste to the sauce.

## Boiling Eggs

This is the best way to perfectly boil an egg. Place eggs in a saucepan and cover with cold water. Bring water to a boil and immediately remove from heat. Cover and let eggs stand in hot water for 10 to 12 minutes. Remove from hot water, cool, peel and chop. Perfect boiled eggs every time.

# Techniques

## Braising

Braising is a wet-heat method of cooking. One benefit of braising is that the liquid absorbs flavors from the foods being braised and makes for a terrific sauce.

Usually, meat or vegetables are first seared in hot fat. Then they are simmered in liquid in a pan with the lid tightly in place. Braising can be done on the stove top or in an oven. The indirect transfer of heat in an oven will cook the food more evenly and is less likely to burn it. Relatively tough cuts of meat benefit from braising - because slow cooking breaks down the tough connective tissues. More tender foods like fish and shellfish may also be braised, but must be cooked for a shorter time at a lower temperature in less liquid.

## Brining

In cooking, brining is a process similar to marination in which meat is soaked in a salt solution (the brine) before cooking. Brining makes cooked meat moister by hydrating the cells of its muscle tissue before cooking, via the process of osmosis, and by allowing the cells to hold onto the water while they are cooked, via the process of denaturation. The brine surrounding the cells has a higher concentration of salt than the fluid within the cells, but the cell fluid has a higher concentration of other solutes. This leads salt ions to enter the cell via diffusion. The increased salinity of the cell fluid causes the cell to absorb water from the brine via osmosis. The salt introduced into the cell also denatures its proteins. The proteins coagulate, forming a matrix which traps water molecules and holds them during cooking. This prevents the meat from drying out, or dehydrating.

A typical brine solution would consist of 1/2 cup kosher salt (1/4 cup if using table salt) to 1 quart of water, plus 3 tablespoons of sugar. The general rule of thumb is 1 hour per pound; however, when brining multiple items the time is based on the weight of a single item. For example if you are brining 4 pork chops, 1 pound each then the brine time would be based on one of the items or 1 pound.

Keep the meat cold during the process with ice surrounding the container, or ice packs placed directly in the water. For small pieces, place inside baggies and refrigerate. Remove from brine solution and rinse thoroughly to remove excess salt and sugar.

Since the brine increases the salt content of the brined object, if you are using the pan juices to create a gravy, you should reduce the salt.

# Appendix A

## Caramelizing Sugar

To start, add some water to dry sugar in a pot, stirring, until it reaches the consistency of wet sand. The acid from added lemon juice will help prevent recrystallization. Instead of using lemon juice, you could add acidity with vinegar, cream of tartar or corn syrup. Always start with a very clean pan and utensils. Any dirt or debris can cause crystals to form around it. Heat the pan over a medium flame. As the sugar melts, you can wash down the sides of a pan with a wet brush, which also prevents crystallization by removing any dried drops of syrup that might start crystals. As the caramel heats, it colors in amber shades from light to deep brown.

## Chiffonade

The French technique of chiffonade, requires cutting into small strips, and is used extensively for fresh herbs. For example, to chiffonade fresh basil, flatten and lay five or six basil leaves on top of each other, and tightly roll them together (like a cigar). Then take a sharp knife and cut across the roll. What you're left with are thin strips of basil leaves. Just perfect to dress up the marinara sauce, you've been wanting to make.

## Clarified Butter

Unsalted butter that has been slowly melted. This causes most of the water and separates the milk solids (which sink to the bottom of the pan) from the golden liquid on the surface. After the foam is skimmed off the top, the clear (clarified) butter is poured or skimmed off the milky residue and used in cooking. Because the milk solids have been removed, clarified butter has a higher smoke point than regular butter and may be used to cook at higher temperatures. In addition, the lack of milk solids prevents clarified butter from becoming rancid as quickly as regular butter. It also means that the butter won't have as rich a flavor. Ghee is an East Indian form of highly clarified butter.

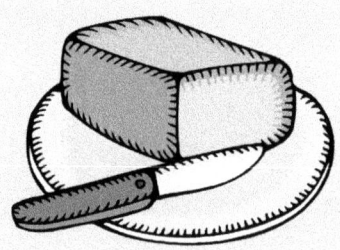

# Techniques

## Emulsify

To emulsify means to combine two liquids that normally do not combine easily, such as oil and vinegar. Emulsifiers are contained in egg white, gelatin, skim milk and mustard. Mayonnaise is a mixture of oil and vinegar or lemon juice that is emulsified by the addition of egg yolk, which contains the emulsifier lecithin.

This is done by slowly adding one ingredient to another while whisking rapidly. This will disperse and suspend one liquid throughout the other. The two liquids will soon separate unless a third ingredient is added; this is called a liaison or emulsifier, which stabilizes the mixture.

## Grill Methods

**Direct**: The method whereby you cook directly over hot coals usually with the cover off to maintain optimum temperature of the coals. This is true grilling because the essence of grilling involves the quick searing of the surface of the food. This ensures good charring and caramelizing the true definition of grilled food.

**Indirect**: Not considered true grilling, more like oven roasting, but performed outdoors in a grill. For this method the coals are heaped on two sides of the grill with an open space between them and often separated by a drip pan. The food is placed in the center of the grill and cooks indirectly with the grill covered to build up enough heat to roast the food.

**Multi-Level**: The process of maintaining different levels of heat in the same grill. This is accomplished by stacking the coals so as to produce two (or more) heat zones. This is ideal for foods that need to be seared over very hot coals then moved to a cooler fire to finish off the cooking.

# Appendix A

## Grilling Non Stick

While most grills are not exactly considered non-stick, there's any easy method that will allow you to cook most items, even fish without fear of sticking.

Before cooking, preheat the grill to high and let it sit covered for a few minutes. Take a wire grill brush, and thoroughly scrape the grill surface. Finally, just before cooking, take a paper towel, soaked with oil, and rub it across the grates.

Set the temperature to whatever your cooking requires, and place the items on the grill. Let the rest a bit before turning; however, you should not experience much if any sticking... Non-stick grilling.

## Julienne

To julienne means to cut into narrow, fine sticks that can measure from 2 to 3 inches long and 1/8 inch square. A finer julienne measures 1/16 of an inch square.

First, determine the length of your julienne and, using your chef's knife, cut the vegetable into pieces. Next, trim the vegetable so its sides are straight and at right angles. Then, holding your knife vertically, slice each piece into 1/8-inch panels. Finally, neatly stack the panels, or lay the panels out on the board, and cut them lengthwise to create uniform matchsticks. Remember to keep your fingers tucked in, and out of the knife's path. For a finer julienne, simply slice thinner panels and thinner matchsticks. A larger matchstick--roughly 1/4 inch across and 2 1/2 inches long, is called a baton.

## Pre-Warming

Although this is not rocket science, pre-warming of plates for the serving of hot foods, can go a long way to keeping things... well, keeping things warm (like I said, this isn't rocket science). There are several commercial brands of plate warmers; everything from equipment that resembles an oven (rather expensive), to flexible devices that resemble a small electric blanket (less expensive).

An easier method, if you aren't using it for anything else, is to heat up your oven to about 130f, and place the plates inside. Of course this method only works if you're planning on serving something hot.

FYI: Avoid pre-warming plates if you're planning to serve ice cream...

Did I mention that this wasn't rocket science.

# Techniques

## Piecrusts

There are four basic ingredients in a piecrust: flour, fat, water and salt. You can come up with numerous variations just by changing your basic ingredients, as long as you stick to the ratio of three parts flour, two parts fat, and one part liquid.

**Flour**: For a tender crust, choose a low-protein flour. Pastry flour, with a protein content of about 8-10%, ranks between all-purpose flour and cake flour. All-purpose flour works just fine for pie crusts, while cake flour may lack enough protein to form a workable, elastic dough. Depending upon your tastes and the recipe, you may substitute nut flours (almond flour or hazelnut flour) or whole-wheat pastry flour for part of the mixture. If you're a novice crust-maker, start with a plain all-purpose or pastry flour dough.

**Fat**: Flaky crusts can be made from a variety of fats. Crusts made with all butter are very flavorful, though they are generally not quite as flaky as crusts made with shortening or lard. Vegetable shortening produces a flaky piecrust that is slightly easier to work with than one made with butter, but the flavor won't be as rich. Lard produces the flakiest crust, but processed lard can have a chemical aftertaste. If you wish to replicate your grandmother's famous piecrust, ask your butcher to order fresh lard.

You can also make a piecrust with vegetable oil. Fans of crispier crusts use melted butter or oil for the fat, resulting in a mealier dough that bakes up in a fine-textured, crisp crust that melts in your mouth. Some of the best piecrusts are made with a combination of fats: half butter, for flavor, and half shortening, for flakiness.

If you're using solid fats (butter, shortening, or lard), they should be kept very cold. When you "cut in" the fat, you want discrete pieces (pea-sized) that don't blend in to the dough as you work it. These flakes of butter will expand and the liquid evaporate during baking, separating the layers of dough into a flaky crust.

# Appendix A

**Liquid**: When adding liquid to the flour and fat mixture, it should be ice-cold in order to keep the pieces of fat cool and separate. Ice water is fine, but fruit juices, egg yolks, sour cream, and milk or cream add different flavors and textures to your piecrust. Always add liquid a tablespoon at a time, tossing with the flour mixture. Humidity can affect dough performance, so you may need less liquid than the recipe calls for. If your dough becomes too wet, you'll need to add more flour to roll out the crust, throwing off your ratio and resulting in a tough crust.

Other additions: Wheat germ, a pinch of spice, a dash of flavorful liqueur or cold brewed coffee are all good additions to piecrusts. Don't forget to add a pinch of salt: the crust will taste flat without it. No matter how good the filling, the crust is the showcase: a good homemade crust takes a pie to new heights. For a sweeter crust, add a tablespoon or two of confectioners' sugar. Granulated sugar can make the dough sticky and harder to work with.

## Pastry Techniques

All ingredients should be ice-cold before mixing.

Do not overwork the dough. Mix quickly and handle the dough as little as possible. Overworking the dough will cause it to be tough.

Chill the dough in the refrigerator for at least 30 minutes before rolling it out. This lets the flour absorb the liquid and helps to prevent stickiness when rolling out the dough. It also allows the gluten (the protein structure) to relax, making it more elastic and less likely to shrink back as you roll it.

Roll the dough out on a lightly floured surface, a pastry cloth, or between two sheets of waxed paper.

Use a dry pastry brush or a clean dish towel to brush off excess flour from the dough.

After the rolled-out dough has been transferred to the pie pan, let it relax in the refrigerator for another 20-30 minutes before filling. This will prevent the dough from shrinking during baking.

Before pouring the filling into the unbaked pie crust, you can brush the bottom and sides of the unbaked pie crust with lightly beaten egg white or melted jelly. This will help create a seal to keep the crust crisp. To ensure that the crust stays even crisper, partially bake the pie crust before adding the filling. (This is, of course, only an option for crumb-topped pies, not latticed or double-crust pies.)

# Techniques

## Pounding Cuts of Meat

Pounding meat cuts to a uniform thickness allows them to cook in a flash. Coat the meat with water, place between two pieces of heavy-duty plastic wrap and pound to a uniform thickness using a meat pounder or the bottom of a heavy skillet. Many meat pounders have two sides, one for pounding and one for tenderizing. Use the smooth side for chicken, as the tenderizing side usually has teeth to break up the tissue in tough cuts of meat.

# Appendix A

## Raft Buildking

Make a raft by first chopping up onions, celery, carrots, and the principal flavoring ingredient (seafood, chicken, beef, or mushrooms depending on what kind of consommé you're making). Mix this with egg whites, salt and pepper and process it in a food processor until very fine. You can use egg whites alone, but the other ingredients boost and fine-tune the flavor of the finished consommé. This first stage is called clearmeat.

Seasonings such as salt and pepper are added to the raft because you don't want to add them to a finished, perfectly clear consommé. The stock itself should also be well seasoned. The clarification process begins by whisking about two cups of cool or warm stock into the raft and then adding this mixture to the rest of the stock. If you've just made your stock and it's still hot, take extra care to whisk the stock, a little at a time, thoroughly with the raft so the heat doesn't coagulate the eggs too soon.

The next step is to bring the whole thing to a gentle simmer over high heat, stirring constantly and gently to prevent the raft from settling at the bottom of the pot and burning which will ruin everything. A good tool to use is a long-handled spatula or flat-ended spoon that will scrape the bottom of the pot. Don't rush this stage if the raft cooks too quickly, it won't take in all of the suspended particles and thoroughly clarify the stock. When the stock reaches a boil, immediately turn down the heat as low as possible while still maintaining a gentle simmer. Stop stirring.

The clearmeat will gradually coagulate and rise to the top as a crust called the "raft". The raft acts as a filter, trapping all the tiny suspended particles as they bubble up through it. Use a ladle or a large spoon to poke a hole in the raft, called a chimney, if a hole doesn't form naturally. The raft will set up better if you baste it occasionally by carefully ladling some stock over it. Don't let the stock boil, which will break up the raft and ruin the clarification of the consommé. After the raft forms, let the stock simmer gently, undisturbed, for about 20 minutes, or until perfectly clear and richly flavored. If the consommé isn't clear after 30 minutes of simmering, most likely the raft has broken up or has stuck to the bottom of the pot. In this case, strain the stock, discard the raft, and begin by making a fresh raft mixture using the same stock.

# Techniques

Now the trick is to retrieve the crystal-clear consommé without mixing up the raft. Just work slowly so you can control the liquids and solids separately. Line a sieve with a clean, damp, lint-free cloth. Ladle the consommé through the lined sieve. Don't try to force the liquid through the sieve, which will only cloud the consommé. When you get down to the bottom of the pot, tilt it over the sieve to pour out all of the free-running consommé; use the ladle to keep the raft from falling out of the pot. Throw away the raft and set the consommé aside to cool, preferably using an ice-bath. Remove any traces of fat from the consommé by blotting the surface with paper towels.

A well-made consommé will be fat-free. It will keep for three days in the refrigerator and up to three months in the freezer.

## Roux (roo)

A mixture of flour and butter used to thicken sauces, soups, and gravies. Most roux are white; made by cooking the flour for only a minute or two. Brown roux—made by cooking the flour until pale brown to dark brown—is also used in many recipes, especially Cajun cooking. It is the basis of three of the five mother sauces of classical French cooking: Béchamel, Velouté, and Espagnole. Butter, vegetable-based oils, or lard are common fats used in the construction of a roux. It is used as a base for gravy, other sauces, Souffles, soups and stews.

A typical roux is created by melting butter (the fat) in a heavy-bottomed pan over medium heat. While the butter is simmering add the flour and whisk until butter and flour form a paste. At this point the chef adds the liquid ingredients such as milk, cream, chicken broth, etc (depending on the type of sauce desired). For example, mixing milk or cream with the roux creates a Sauce béchamel, adding a light chicken, veal, or fish stock to the roux would create a Sauce velouté, and adding several gallons of veal stock or water, along with 20–30 lb (9–14 kg) of browned bones, pieces of beef, many pounds of vegetables, and various seasonings to a very dark brown roux, is the basis for a Sauce Espagnole.

A dark roux will thicken less than light roux.

If black specks appear in the roux, it has burned and you'll have to start over.

If the roux is made ahead and refrigerated, pour excess oil from the surface before reheating, or let it return to room temperature

# Appendix A

## Recipe for a typical roux

Melt 1/2 cup (unless a specific amount is called for) of butter, shortening, oil, or other fat in a heavy skillet over very low heat.

Gradually sprinkle the hot melted fat with the same proportion of flour and immediately begin stirring.

Stir the mixture constantly until it reaches the desired color, which may take from 15 to 30 minutes.

Remove from the heat and continue stirring until it has cooled down a bit and there's no risk of burning.

Add to whatever your recipe calls for, or store roux tightly covered in the refrigerator for later use.

## Saute (saw-TAY):

To cook food quickly in a small amount of fat or oil, until brown, in a skillet or saute pan over direct heat. The saute pan and fat must be hot before the food is added, otherwise the food will absorb oil and become soggy.

To cook food quickly in oil or fat. Similar to the word fry, but sautéing uses a smaller amount of oil or fat.

By the way, saute means "jump" in French and is named for the tossing technique used to keep the food moving and evenly cooked.

## Skinning a Pepper

1. Preheat the oven to 375° F.

2. In a bowl toss the pepper with the olive oil. Transfer to a baking sheet and bake for 10 minutes.

3. Turn the pepper over and cook for another 10 minutes until completely soft.

4. Remove the pepper from oven. Transfer to a bowl and cover with plastic wrap; or seal it in a plastic storage bag, and set aside for 10 minutes.

Note: This trick will aid in the removal of the pepper's skin.

5. Remove the pepper, and when it is cool enough to handle, remove as much of the skin as possible along with the stem and seeds.

# Techniques

# Appendix B

This section is dedicated to cooking terminology, like what does boil, blanch, or dice mean. No big deal; however, if you get stuck on a specific term, hopefully it will be listed on the following pages.

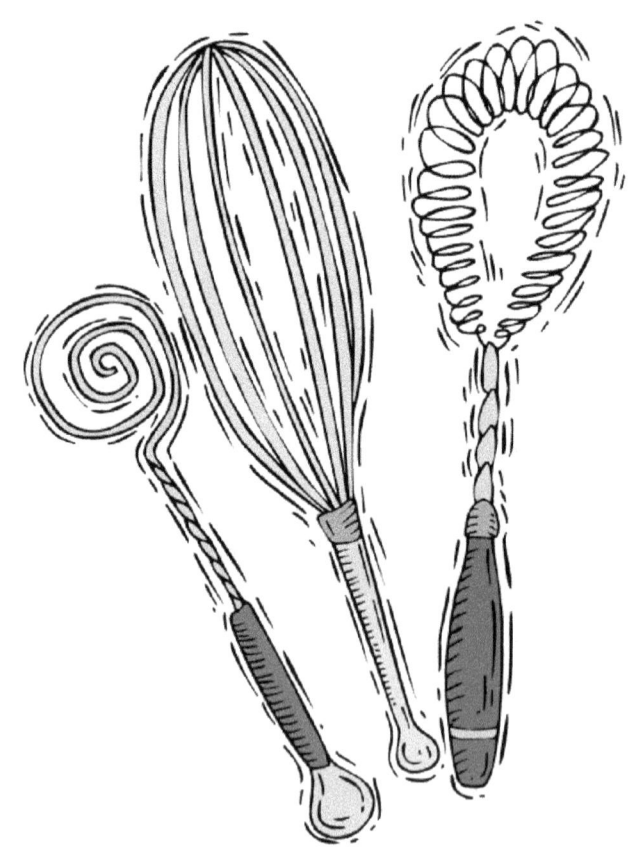

# Terminology

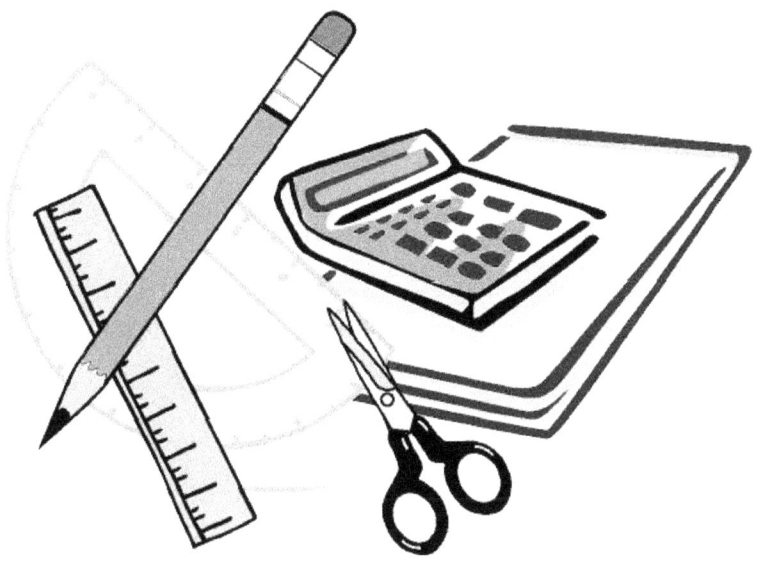

# Appendix B: Terminology

### AERATE
To pass dry ingredients through a fine-mesh sifter so large pieces can be removed. The process also incorporates air to make ingredients like flour, lighter. Sifting dry ingredients aerates them while distributing small amounts of chemical leaveners or dry seasoning evenly through the mixture. Use sifters, sieves or tamis to both aerate and sift.

### Al Dente
Meaning "to the bite." Literally "to the tooth," used to describe the correct degree of doneness for pasta and vegetables. This is not exactly a procedure, but a sensory evaluation for deciding when the food is finished cooking. Pasta should retain a slight resistance when biting into it, but should not have a hard center. For the best flavor, cook your pasta until it is firm and chewy.

### BASTE
To brush or spoon food as it cooks with melted fat or the cooking juices from the dish. Basting prevents foods from drying out and adds color and flavor.

### BLANCH
To cook raw ingredients in boiling water briefly. Blanched vegetables are generally "shocked" by plunging immediately and briefly into an ice water bath to stop the cooking process and preserve color and crunch. Blanching and shocking are useful in removing the skins of some fruits and vegetables.

### BLEND
To combine two or more ingredients together with a spoon, beater or blender.

### BOIL
To heat a liquid to its boiling point, until bubbles break the surface. "Boil" also means to cook food in a boiling liquid.

### BOUQUET GARNI
A bundle of herbs and spices used for flavoring but removed before serving. Usually includes parsley, thyme and bay leaves. May be secured in cheesecloth or just tied together at the stem ends. A tea ball works well for crushed herbs and spices. The classic bouquet garni consists of a few bay leaves, a parsley sprig and a thyme sprig tied in cheesecloth.

# Aerate to Chop

### BRAISE
To cook food, tightly covered, in a small amount of liquid at low heat for a long period of time. Sometimes, the food is first browned in fat. The long, slow cooking tenderizes meats by gently breaking down their fibers. The braising liquid keeps meats moist and can be used as a basis for sauce. Use wine, stocks or water as components in braising liquid.

### BROIL
To cook food directly above or under a heat source. Food can be broiled in an oven or on a grill.

### BROTH
Liquid in which meat, fish, cereal grains, or vegetables (no bones) have been simmered and strained out. Broth is used as a basis for soup, gravy, or sauce. It is very flavorful and can be eaten alone or with garnish.

### BUTTERFLY
To split food (meat, fish, fowl) down the center, cutting almost, but not completely through. The two halves are then opened flat to resemble a butterfly.

### CHIFFONADE
To slice into very thin strips or shreds. Literally translated from French, the term means "made of rags."

### CHOP
To cut food into bite-size pieces using a knife. A food processor may also be used to chop food. Chopped food is more coarsely cut than minced food.

# Appendix B: Terminology

### CLARIFY

To remove sediment from a cloudy liquid, thereby making it clear. To clarify liquids, such as stock, egg whites and/or eggshells are commonly added and simmered for approximately 15 minutes. The egg whites attract and trap particles from the liquid. After cooling, strain the mixture through a cloth-lined sieve to remove residue. To clarify rendered fat, add hot water and boil for about 15 minutes. The mixture should then be strained through several layers of cheesecloth and chilled. The resulting layer of fat should be completely clear of residue.: Clarified butter is butter that has been heated slowly so that its milk solids separate and sink, and can be discarded. The resulting clear liquid can be used at a higher cooking temperature and will not go rancid as quickly as unclarified butter.

### DEGLAZE

To remove browned bits of food from the bottom of a pan after sauteing, usually meat. After the food and excess fat have been removed from the pan, a small amount of liquid is heated with the cooking juices in the pan and stirred to remove browned bits of food from the bottom. The resulting mixture often becomes the base for a sauce.

### DEGORGE

To sprinkle vegetables with salt to eliminate water. Eggplant for example are generally salted and patted dry before cooking.

### DICE

To cut food into tiny cubes (about 1/8- to 1/4-inch).

### DRAIN

To pour off fat or liquid from food, often using a colander.

### DREDGE

To lightly coat food that is going to be fried with flour, breadcrumbs or cornmeal. The coating helps to brown the food and provides a crunchy surface. Dredged foods need to be cooked immediately, while breaded foods, those dredged in flour, dipped in egg then dredged again in breading, can be prepared and held before cooking.

# Clarify to Grill

**EMULSIFY**

To bind together two liquid ingredients that normally do not combine smoothly, such as water and fat. Slowly add one ingredient to the other while mixing rapidly. This action disperses tiny droplets of one liquid in the other. Mayonnaise and vinaigrettes are emulsions. Use a good whisk for steady, even emulsification.

**FILLET**

To create a fillet of fish or meat by cutting away the bones. Fish and boning knives help produce clean fillets.

**FOLD**

To combine a light mixture like beaten egg whites with a much heavier mixture like whipped cream. In a large bowl, place the lighter mixture on top of the heavier one. Starting at the back of the bowl, using the edge of a rubber spatula, cut down through the middle of both mixtures, across the bottom of the bowl and up the near side. Rotate the bowl a quarter turn and repeat. This process gently combines the two mixtures.

**FRY**

To cook food (non-submerged) in hot fat or oil over moderate to high heat. There is very little difference between frying and SAUTEING although sauteing is often thought of as being faster and using less fat.

**GRATE**

To reduce a large piece of food to coarse or fine threads by rubbing it against a rough, serrated surface, usually on a grater. A food processor, fitted with the appropriate blades, can also be used for grating. The food that is being grated should be firm. Cheese that needs to be grated can be refrigerated first for easier grating.

**GRILL**

To cook food on a grill over hot coals or other heat source. The intense heat creates a crust on the surface of the food which seals in the juices. The grill should be clean and must be heated before the food is laid on it. The food can also be basted and seasoned.

# Appendix B: Terminology

### GRIND
To reduce food to small pieces by running it through a grinder. Food can be ground to different degrees, from fine to coarse.

### HOMOGENIZE
To create an emulsion by reducing all the particles to the same size. The fat globules are broken down mechanically until they are evenly distributed throughout the liquid. Homogenized milk and some commercial salad dressings are two examples of homogenized foods.

### INFUSE
To steep an aromatic ingredient in hot liquid until the flavor has been extracted and absorbed by the liquid. Teas are infusions. Milk or cream can also be infused with flavor before being used in custards or sauces.

### JULIENNE
To cut food into thin sticks. Food is cut with a knife or mandoline into even slices, then into strips.

### KNEAD
To mix and work dough into a smooth, elastic mass. Kneading can be done either manually or by machine. By hand, kneading is done with a pressing-folding-turning action. First the dough is pressed with the heels of both hands and pushed away from the body so the dough stretches out. The dough is then folded in half, given a quarter turn, and the process is repeated. Depending on the dough, the kneading time can range anywhere from 5 to 15 minutes. During kneading, the gluten strands stretch and expand, enabling dough to hold in gas bubbles formed by a leavener, which allows it to rise.

### MARINATE
To soak food in a seasoned liquid mixture for a certain length of time. The purpose of marinating is to add flavor and/or tenderize the food. Due to the acidic ingredients in many marinades, foods should be marinated in glass, ceramic or stainless steel containers. Foods should also be covered and refrigerated while they are marinating. When fruits are soaked in this same manner, the process is called macerating.

# Grind to Mirepoix

## MANGO

The mango is represented by 35 species of tropical fruiting trees, that are native to India and Indochina. Mangos were introduced to California (Santa Barbara) in 1880. The tree is long-lived with some specimens known to be over 300 years old, and still fruiting. Mangoes grow in a wide variety of shapes (oblong, kidney and round) and sizes (from about 6 ounces to 4 pounds). Their thin, tough skin is green and, as the fruit ripens, becomes yellow with red mottling. The flesh is a golden orange, juicy and wonderfully sweet and tart. Perhaps the only negative to the mango is the huge, flat seed that traverses its length. The fruit must be carefully carved away from the seed with a sharp knife.

Mangos luxuriate in summer heat and resent cool summer fog. Hence the best mangos are cultivated in the mid to latter part of the Summer months.

## MASH

To crush a food into smooth and evenly textured state. For potatoes or other root vegetables, use a ricer, masher or food mill. While food processors provide a smooth texture more like a puree or a paste, they should not be used for potatoes.

## MINCE

To cut food into very tiny pieces. Minced food is cut into smaller, finer pieces than diced food.

## MIREPOIX (mihr-PWAH)

Mixed finely diced vegetables, typically carrot, onion, and celery, lightly fried and used as a seasoning in stews, soups, and sauces, or on which to lay meat for roasting or braising. Named after the late 19th century French diplomat and general, the Duc de Mirepoix, 1699-1757.

# Appendix B: Terminology

## MOTHER SAUCE

First, let's define the term sauce. In cooking, a sauce (not gravy) is a liquid or sometimes semi-solid food served on or used in preparing other foods. Sauces are not a dish in themselves; they add flavor, moisture, and visual appeal to other dishes. Sauce is a French word taken from the Latin salsus, meaning salted. Sauces need a liquid component, but with dishes such as pasta can contain more solid elements than liquid. A person who specializes in making sauces is often referred to as a "saucier". It's a French term... the French think of everything.

**Mother Sauces**: In the early 20th century, the chef Auguste Escoffier classified what he called the five "mother" sauces in cooking: Béchamel, Espagnole, Hollandaise, Tomato sauce, and Velouté. Escoffier's schema is still taught to chefs today.

- **Veloute** - Stock thickened with roux.
- **Bechamel** - Milk thickened with roux
- **Tomato** - Sauces with a tomato base.
- **Espagnole** - Brown sauce, made with roux, veal stock, roasted veal bones and mirepoix.
- **Hollandaise** - Heated egg yolk and clarified butter.

The "Mother" sauces are the base or beginning of other sauces. In other words, you would make the Mother Sauce, and then go on to make other sauces.

## MOUNT

To whisk cold butter, piece by piece, into a warm sauce for smooth texture, flavor and sheen. Each piece of butter must be thoroughly incorporated before a new piece is added so that the sauce does not break (or separate into liquid and fat).

## NAP

To completely coat food with a light, thin, even layer of sauce.

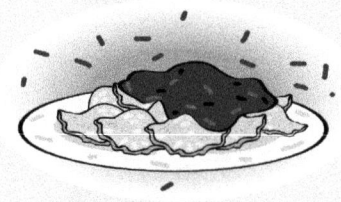

# Mother Sauce to Quadriller

**PARBOIL**

To boil food briefly in water, cooking it only partially. Parboiling is used for dense food like carrots and potatoes. After being parboiled, these foods can be added at the last minute to quicker-cooking ingredients. Parboiling insures that all ingredients will finish cooking at the same time. Since foods will continue to cook once they have been removed from the boiling water, they should be shocked in ice water briefly to preserve color and texture. Cooking can then be completed by sautéing or the parboiled vegetable can be added to simmering soups or stews.

**PARE**

To remove the thin outer layer of foods using a paring knife or a vegetable peeler.

**PEEL**

To remove the rind or skin from a fruit or vegetable using a knife or vegetable peeler.

**POACH**

To cook food by gently simmering in liquid at or just below the boiling point. The amount of the liquid and poaching temperature depends on the food being poached.

**PUREE**

To grind or mash food until completely smooth. This can be done using a food processor or blender or by pressing the food through a sieve.

**QUADRILLER**

To mark the surface of grilled or broiled food with a crisscross pattern of lines. The scorings are produced by contact with very hot single grill bars which brown the surface of the food. Very hot skewers may also be used to mark the surface.

# Appendix B: Terminology

### RASPBERRY (RAZ-behr-ee)
Considered by many the most intensely flavored member of the berry family. There are three main varieties-black, golden and red, the latter being the most widely available. Depending on the region, raspberries are available from May through November. Choose brightly colored, plump berries sans hull. If the hulls are still attached, the berries were picked too early and will undoubtedly be tart. Avoid soft, shriveled or moldy berries. Store (preferably in a single layer) in a moisture proof container in the refrigerator for 2 to 3 days. If necessary, rinse lightly just before serving. Raspberries contain a fair amount of iron, potassium and vitamins A and C.

And one other thing... A raspberry can be a derisive sounds of disapproval; such as a boo, catcall, hiss, or hoot. Now, aren't you glad you read this definition.

### REDUCE
To thicken or concentrate a liquid by boiling rapidly. The volume of the liquid is reduced as the water evaporates, thereby thickening the consistency and intensifying the flavor.

### RICE
To push cooked food through a perforated kitchen tool called a ricer. The resulting food looks like rice.

### ROAST
To oven-cook food in an uncovered pan. The food is exposed to high heat which produces a well-browned surface and seals in the juices. Reasonably tender pieces of meat or poultry should be used for roasting.

### SCALD
To dip fruits or vegetables in boiling water in order to loosen their skins and simplify peeling. The produce should be left in the water for only 30 seconds to prohibit cooking, and should be shocked in an ice water bath before the skin is removed

# Raspberry to Sift

### SEAR
To brown meat or fish quickly over very high heat either in a fry pan, under a broiler or in a hot oven. Searing seals in the food's juices and provides a crisp tasty exterior. Seared food can then be eaten rare or roasted or braised to desired degree of doneness.

### SEASON
To add flavor to foods, or to coat the cooking surface of a new pot or pan with vegetable oil then heat in a 350 degree oven for about an hour. This smooths out the surface of new pots and pans, particularly cast-iron, and prevents foods from sticking.

### SHOCKING
The process of plunging a fruit or vegetable into ice water; typically after first placing the item in boiling water (called blanching). Shocking is used for several purposes. For example, the classic method for cooking broccoli, asparagus, carrots, and so on, usually consists of two steps. The first is blanching in hot water for a few minutes, between one and five. Then the vegetable is shocked quickly and briefly in ice cold water. After that the vegetable is left to rest for a minute or two. Finally, it is cooked by some other method which may be sauteing, steaming, or something else entirely.

Another purpose is to assist in the removal of the fruit or vegetable's skin. For example, blanching tomatoes for about 1 minute, and then shocking them, helps to easily remove the skin. This is invaluable in the creation of a tomato sauce.

### SIEVE
To strain liquids or particles of food through a sieve or strainer. Press the solids, using a ladle or wooden spoon, into the strainer to remove as much liquid and flavor as possible.

### SIFT
To pass dry ingredients through a fine mesh sifter so large pieces can be removed. The process also incorporates air to make ingredients like flour, lighter. Synonymous with AERATE.

# Appendix B: Terminology

### SIMMER

To bring a liquid almost to a boil over low heat. Simmering liquid is characterized by small bubbles which rise slowly to the surface, usually breaking before they reach the surface.

### SKIM

To remove the scum that rises to the surface from a liquid when it is boiled. The top layer of the liquid, such as the cream from milk or the foam and fat from stock, soups or sauces, can be removed using a spoon, ladle or skimmer. Soups, stews or sauces can be chilled so that the fat coagulates on the surface and may be easily removed before reheating.

### Spices (dried)

Dried spices lack the essential oils present in fresh; however, they have a tendency to be about 50 percent more potent. Therefore, if a recipe calls for fresh, and you only have dry, reduce the amount accordingly.

In addition, most dried spices do not last much more than six months. Yet, if I were to look into most spice cabinets I would most likely see spice bottles that date back to the Civil War. When you cook with old spices, you're not cooking with flavor, you're cooking with dust. Examine your spices and retire the ones with dates older than six months... please.

### STEAM

To cook food on a rack or in steamer basket over a boiling liquid in a covered pan. Steaming retains flavor, shape, texture, and nutrients better than boiling or poaching.

### STOCK

Stock, is made from bones (chicken, fish beef, veal), which along with the vegetables, give their life to the stock, simmering in the liquid for hours. Whereas, broth is make without the bones. Differences in taste between a stock and broth cannot be overstated.

# Simmer to Zest

### SWEAT
To cook vegetables in fat over gentle heat so they become soft but not brown, and their juices are concentrated in the cooking fat. If the pan is covered during cooking, the ingredients will keep a certain amount of their natural moisture. If the pan is not covered, the ingredients will remain relatively dry.

### TENDERIZE
To make meat more tender by pounding with a mallet, marinating for varying periods of time, or storing at lower temperatures. Fat may also be placed into a piece of meat to make it more tender during cooking.

### TRUSS
To secure food, usually poultry or game, with string, pins or skewers so that it maintains a compact shape during cooking. Trussing allows for easier basting during cooking.

### UNLEAVENED
The word which describes any baked good that has no leavener, such as yeast, baking powder or baking soda.

### WHIP
To beat ingredients such as egg whites or cream until light and fluffy. Air is incorporated into the ingredients as they are whipped, increasing their volume until they are light and fluffy.

### WHISK
To beat ingredients together until smooth, using a kitchen tool called a whisk.

### XXX, XXXX, 10X
An indicator on a box of confectioners sugar of how many times it has been ground. The higher the number of X's the finer the grind.

### ZEST
To remove the outermost skin layers of citrus fruit using a knife, peeler or zester. When zesting, be careful not to remove the pith, the white layer between the zest and the flesh, which is bitter

# Appendix C

*This section has a few examples of recipe cards, shopping lists, and flow charts. Like all organizational schemes, the point is to pick a method that is comfortable to your particular organization style. If it isn't, you won't use it.*

# Resources

# Appendix C: Resources

**SIDE 1**

Recipe for: _____  Serves: _____

_____
_____
_____
_____
_____
_____
_____
_____
_____

Type: _____  Code: _____

**SIDE 2**

Ingredients

_____
_____
_____
_____
_____
_____
_____
_____

Ingredients

_____
_____
_____
_____
_____
_____
_____
_____

# Recipe Cards

# Appendix C: Resources

Recipe: _____
From the Kitchen of: _____

_____
_____
_____
_____
_____
_____
_____
_____

Recipe: _____
From the Kitchen of: _____

_____
_____
_____
_____
_____
_____
_____
_____

# Recipe Cards

Recipe: _____
From the Kitchen of: _____
_____
_____
_____
_____
_____
_____
_____
_____
_____
_____

Recipe: _____
From the Kitchen of: _____
_____
_____
_____
_____
_____
_____
_____
_____
_____
_____

# Appendix C: Resources

## SHOPPING LIST

## SHOPPING LIST

# Shopping Lists

# Appendix C: Resources

## Cooking Flow Chart

| 12 | 1 | 2 | 3 | 4 | 5 | 6 | 7 | 8 | 9 | 10 | 11 |
|----|---|---|---|---|---|---|---|---|---|----|----|
|    |   |   |   |   |   |   |   |   |   |    |    |

12: _____
1: _____
2: _____
3: _____
4: _____
5: _____
6: _____
7: _____
8: _____
9: _____
10: _____
11: _____

# Flowcharts

I've always thought of a flowchart as what ever you wanted it to look like. When I've cooked in restaurants as a line chef, the flowchart is part of the daily routine that's burned into your brain. And, depending on the size of the restaurant, you might have prep chefs, and plating chefs helping in the process.

At school, the form of the flowchart is determined by your instructor/chef; however, with home entertaining, you're pretty much left to your own devices (that's not such a bad thing).

Typically, I jot down some notes on when the potatoes go to boil, or when I need to put the Parker House rolls into the oven. These notes then get stuck to the vent fan over my cooking area. The whole idea is to have everything come out at the same time... that's the idea, anyway.

So, come up with a plan, chart, flowchart... whatever you want to call it. Then get in that kitchen and have the time of your life.

## Kitchen Planner

| Time | Task |
|------|------|
|      |      |

| Time    |   | Task                        |
|---------|---|-----------------------------|
| 8:00am  | - | Pick up salmon              |
| 9:15am  | - | Place salmon into marinade  |
| 12:00pm | - | Set up dinning area         |
| 12:30pm | - | Make first set of quiches   |
| 1:30pm  | - | Make second set of quiches  |
| . . . . . . . . . . . . . |   |                             |

# In Conclusion

There is no conclusion (there is no spoon).

How can there be a conclusion to a book that deals with cooking. Cooking is an art form that is not perfect; however, it's proven that over time it can be perfected. For example, I've never met a recipe that I didn't like (honest). But like all recipes, they can be changed… a dash of this, and a pinch of that, and you've taken a great recipe and made it a bit of you, along with your likes and dislikes.

If you take anything away from this book, take away the fact that the culinary arts evolve with the times, and that it's you that assists in that evolution. As your skills grow, so will your desire to reach out and try new and unique techniques and dishes. That is what it's all about.

Just remember, eating is about gathering together with friends and family, and sharing that joy with others.

Enjoy this marvelous gift of life that we've been so graciously given, and share that gift with others… preferably over a plate of food.

Share the joy and enjoy the journey.

*Andy Anderson*

Keep the Faith... And Keep Cooking

www.ingramcontent.com/pod-product-compliance
Ingram Content Group UK Ltd.
Pitfield, Milton Keynes, MK11 3LW, UK
UKHW050411240426
12048UKWH00020B/1452